T0368398

REVELATORY

WORDS FOR ANY GIVEN DAY

CARD OR SERIES TITLE PAGE

365 REVELATORY

WORDS FOR ANY GIVEN DAY

DAILY DEVOTIONAL
FOR THE SEEKERS OF TRUE REVELATION

DR. JENNIFER GILBERT

365 REVELATORY WORDS FOR ANY GIVEN DAY
DAILY DEVOTIONAL FOR THE SEEKERS OF TRUE REVELATION

Scripture quotations marked KJV are from the Holy Bible, King James Version (Authorized Version). First published in 1611. Quoted from the KJV Classic Reference Bible, Copyright © 1983 by The Zondervan Corporation.

iUniverse books may be ordered through booksellers or by contacting:

iUniverse
1663 Liberty Drive
Bloomington, IN 47403
www.iuniverse.com
1-800-Authors (1-800-288-4677)

ISBN: 978-1-5320-2466-5 (sc)
ISBN: 978-1-5320-2465-8 (e)

Library of Congress Control Number: 2017910140

Print information available on the last page.

iUniverse rev. date: 08/02/2017

For everyone who is looking for a deeper revelation of the word of God without the typical layout of scripture and three points and a poem, but revelatory revelation of what is really going on in this current day and time in a manner in which they can actively participate. This book is for you.

Almighty God, thank you for favoring me with the gift of words and interpretation, but most of all the gift of revelation. I thank you now for loving me in spite of me and the foolish things I have done, may currently do and the silly things to come. You are my peace and I worship you. To my children, we did it again. Thanks so much for your love and support. I cannot do all this without you. To life who has taught me so many lessons and gave me greater degrees of education than any institution of higher learning can give, I honor you. To every person that has touched my life in anyway; I want to say thanks for your contribution. To my mother, Orelia Marie Richardson-Johnson, for the painful lessons that you taught me, I know you gave me only what you knew how to give, and though at times I felt it wasn't enough or it wasn't right, I know now it was more than enough. To my earthly father, Lester Adams, though you were absent when I thought it was most important, I bless God for placing you in my life when it is truly most important, NOW!

EPIGRAPH

The revelatory reveals what is often disdained in the reading of the scripture. It is the deeper understanding of the message to be used as a revolutionary force for your deliverance and understanding

CONTENTS

FOREWORD BY
DR. DONALD STALLINGS

Whether you are new or a mature Christian, you will find practical and useful information within the covers of this workbook. Each daily devotional expounds upon real life events and through some of Dr. Gilbert's own personal experiences. She has done an excellent job in sharing her stories and giving us practical application of the word and how it relates to us in modern times. Through each page of this book, one would discover how profound the influence of the word of God is in their daily lives. This workbook explores practical application to challenges that people face on a daily basis. The inspiration of this book comes from the author's willingness to take on topics that many Christians and Non-Christians find challenging, but unwillingly want to tackle head. For the non-Christians, this workbook would show that Christians and Non-Christians face similar changes, but the difference is how Christians use the word of God to help them to navigate through these challenges. Also, this workbook challenges the reader to think and reflect on real life situations and how they can overcome them. So many times people think they are the only one who is facing challenges, but this book shares with it readers that they are not alone in trying to navigate through life's challenges and there is hope.

As you read the daily devotionals, remember that you will learn more from the experiences written in each devotional that could help you to navigate through your own personal challenges, or avoid them all together. Remember, the best thing about a book like this that Dr. Gilbert has written, it allows you not only to learn, but to journal your own personal stories along-side of each devotional. You will learn and grow at the same time through the experiences of others.

PREFACE

This is not your ordinary devotional book. I wish that in all of my books that the reader is not just reading, but participating in the experience that they are embarking upon. I believe the more interactive the material, the more meaningful the experience.

ACKNOWLEDGEMENTS

To life and all of the ups and downs that are entailed. Thanks for teaching me what no man, woman, boy, or girl could teach me. To the many times I thought of shortening your timespan, thanks for easing up just enough to let me see that I can survive yet another trial, and yes this too will pass. To life, for showing me the strength that others wouldn't, couldn't, or just didn't take the time to explore or exemplify. Thanks to life for all the people that you allowed in and out of you so that I can see who is who in the universe that we call a world. To life, who taught me the difference between family and kindred, friends and foes, failure and fatalities, in all instances one is temporary and the other is forever. I honor you, life!

INTRODUCTION

We all have those days where we just need a pick me up. A day when it seems like you just need a simple word. A getaway, a reprieve from the day to day struggles we call life. That is what this book is meant to be for you. A simple revelatory way of connecting with God and hearing what he has to say versus you being preached at with the normal scripture with three points and a poem.

Though this book is entitled 365 Revelatory Words for Any Given Day…this devotional can be read in any order and at any time. There is even an extra day placed inside for leap years. Some of the devotionals have scriptures, but for the most part they are just revelatory words that God just dropped in my spirit in an effort to encourage my readers. I pray that you are blessed beyond measure in this literary experience.

Day 1

JOURNALING FOR JESUS

What are you writing in your journal? Is it revelation that will help you in later situations or is it a homage to your "woe is me" syndrome? David shows us the need to encourage ourselves. Our visitation to our journals should not depress us, nor tell us how we got over the rough side of the mountain, but should be filled with revelation of the lessons that God wants us to learn from the experience he just delivered us from. This way when we revisit it, it can serve as a form of self-encouragement and edification that propels us to move forward from where we are, to where we should be.

Many attribute their journaling to the advisement of Oprah, but if the truth be told journaling began back in the Bible days wherein the gospels were written to encourage others and to speak of an account. Journaling is such a powerful venture that even Jesus commonly quoted, "it is written…" which was spoken to proclaim and/or reclaim order.

Your personal journal should serve the same purpose, reclaim and/or proclaim order and bring the sanity back to your remembrance of the former days when God brought you through that so you will understand that God IS the same YESTERDAY, TODAY AND FOREVERMORE!

As you write your personal reflections of this book, I encourage you write words that are empowering and encouraging and that bring life to your situation if ever you choose to read it on a less than pleasant day. Be mindful of the words that you speak, even in your writing. Remember that Apostle Paul wrote letters that changed the lives of many and so should the words that you write.

THINK AHEAD OF THE ENEMY

I am sitting here in L.A. and I am listening to all of these record execs and the like and I am thinking to myself, "Besides the thickness of their pockets, what is the different between them and me?" The biggest difference between them and me is that I have the Holy Ghost and the anointing...As I sit here and watch them strategize my life for me I understand that God has the FINAL say...I am reminded of Daniel in the Lion's den...Do you want to know why he wasn't eaten by the lions? Good, I'm glad you asked! Lol... Daniel went on a fast prior to the turn of events that propelled him into his destiny and because of his obedience (no meat) the lion's didn't even eat him because he didn't have IN him what ATTRACTED them. Lions are meat eaters (carnivores) not herbivores (vegetable eaters)...Daniel thought ahead of the enemy and knew what his destiny would be, so he prepared himself for the storm before it came...How can we better prepare ourselves for the storms that are coming in our life that are here to propel us into our destiny? We have to make sure that we have THE WORD in us that will cover us inside and out as we go through our storms and no matter what the outsiders say it's what is on the inside that counts. WATCH YOU'RE INSIDE MOTIVATION BECAUSE IT WILL EFFECT YOUR OUTSIDE SITUATION!

DAY 3

ELEVATION AND ESCALATION?

Elevation does not come easy. You have to do some work. When in the larger malls, there are normally a set of stairs and a set of escalators. Just by default, many choose the escalator because it doesn't require any real effort or energy. We actually think in our minds for that reason that it's easier and quicker. Kingdom solidified elevation does not happen that way and if it did, it would be short lived because you would not be fit to function in your calling. Why? I'm glad you asked. You would not be fit to function because you did not do any work to gain the foundational knowledge and skills that it takes to perform the many tasks that come with spiritual elevation. Fitness comes from persevering through the pains of pressurizing the muscles that testify to the fruits of your labor but without the pressure there will be no fruits and without fruits there can be no elevation.

In the days of quick weight loss mania, there are all kinds of methods from shots to pills, to lap bands, gastric bypasses and the like, but nothing compares to the old school form of working out and discipline because it is the only true source of labor that is proven to stand the test of time. So it is with the spiritual portion of our lives. Many people want to walk into the limelight of Christendom and become the heavy hitters like T.D. Jakes and the like, but don't realize the work out and discipline that it took to become who they are. Many of them were individuals who had no choice but to take the stairs to elevation and not the escalator. It is what the old people call the road less traveled. This is why the Bible speaks of working out your own soul salvation. It is just that, a work out and not a hookup.

The Bible tells us not to despise the days of humble beginnings. So what if you start off small. I don't know anyone who has been successful for any length of time that go to their level of success quickly; it all started small like our muscles and grew as we worked out our own soul salvation.

Day 4

WHAT IS YOUR ADDRESS?

Psalm 91:1
*He that dwelleth in the secret place of the most High shall **abide under** the **shadow** of the Almighty.*

To be powerful and prolific you have to have patience and perseverance otherwise your prophetic word can become a pathetic word that does more hurting than healing. True prophetic revelation only comes from abiding (living) in HIS presence! Question: Where do you live?

The place in which you choose to abide can and will determine your destination. If you choose to live in sin, then your ultimate destination is hell. If you choose to live a lifestyle of holiness and truth, then your ultimate destination should be heaven (provided you've completed the plan of salvation).

The true question is where are you abiding right now? The Bible says, he who dwells in the shelter of the most high shall abide under the shadow of the almighty. Take shelter in the arms of Christ wherein you can experience the peace that passes all understanding. No matter what storms come and go your peace will be sustained.

Only in a state of peace can you truly hear the still, small voice that is the Holy Ghost which will make your word more weighted than anything else you can offer the body of Christ. The prophetic anointing is one that focuses on the giving portion of the five-fold. They are there to give guidance and direction, but if their head is cluttered and their world is crazy it is more likely that their words will be tainted because they can become entangled with personal thoughts and opinions. Clear your head, clear your heart, clear your prophesy.

Day 5

PROSTRATION OR PACIFY?

<u>**1 Corinthians 1**</u> (entire chapter)

As Christians we need to understand time and season…there are times when God will tell us to pacify a person with an issue as an exemplification of love and compassion (milk), but after you have suffered a while, there comes a mandate of action and accountability (prostration) wherein we are to labor with the individual with a firm hand of correction (meat) that takes them from destruction to destiny. The problem is we have a lot of people attending the course without their parental permission slip from the father. What does this mean? It means that there are people who are "called", people who are "sent" and then there are those who just "went". We don't know the difference because they all look the same and have the same hunger for knowledge, but it goes back to the intent or motive of their hunger. The "called" are hungry because they are mandated by God to attain the knowledge to lead the people. The "sent" are called because they understand that in order to go they have to grow. The "went" are hungry for selfish gain. Where the word says to study to show thyself approved, they study to prove themselves which in turn causes them to use their knowledge to operate in witchcraft or to get people to see things their way when their way is clearly not the way of the father. How can we know the difference? Watch their works and if they don't have a parental permission slip from our heavenly father to attend the course by the deadline, we have to leave them behind no looking back. We are spending too much time on the aint's and the saints are suffering because the "called" and the "sents" are being camouflaged by the "wents".

Check the lives of your leadership, but first check your own life and try the spirit by the spirit and see if it is of God

Day 6

WHO IS ME?

The first song that I ever wrote alone and personally recorded was entitled, "Can I Just Be Me?" Of course we know hindsight is 20/20. As an extension to that thought, I am left with the question of who is "Me"? Many of us go through an identity crisis in life on more than one occasion…Some think that it happens during the teens and even preteens, then they came up with the stigma of a midlife crisis. I would like to lend a thought to the matter that we are continually experiencing an identity crisis when we are in the will of God because daily we die to our flesh and with each death and burial; there is a resurrection of something new and different that God will have us to embark upon. So if we are willing and obedient to the voice of the master, we are forever changing which means just when I think I know "me," "me" changes into someone more like "thee" so in all actuality there is never a "me" to be because I have to be close to "thee" to know "ME."

Day 7

MAN + WOMAN

Man =Power, Woman=Influence,
Man + Woman = Dominion

One day I was having a conversation with Pastor Terri Ross and we were talking about my observation of how in most marriages I see, it appears as though the woman is always in control, but they do this thing called "acts of submission" that in reality seems like an act of kindness of some sort to make the man feel as though he is in control and I told her that I did not want that type of relationship, that I wanted it to be a true role. I told her that if I was going to submit, I wanted someone to authentically submit to. She gave me the powerful equation above (not sure if it's an original thought or not) however, it does mirror the likeness of the role of man and woman.

When conception takes place the woman is the carrier of the initial X chromosome, but the man adds the additional X or Y to make the seed a male or female child. Yes, the male does have the power (innately) to determine the gender, and the female is more influential on the life of the growing embryo, but, ultimately it takes both of them to make the child and each plays their role, but the rearing of the child is again where both parties are needed.

This principle also rings true in the body of Christ. We, as women, are birthers or nurturers and men are seed planters. They are to have the vision and we are to be the ones to help birth that vision. Oftentimes, the issue is that someone drops that ball, thus causing for the fatalities in today's marriages. Either the man forsakes the vision, or the lady refuses to support it which creates an imbalance and ultimately another matrimonial fatality.

Check your role in the relationship that you are in and make sure that you are authentic in your actions and that your motives are pure and that what you are birthing is not a product of confusion and dysfunction.

RELATIONSHIP WITHIN RELIGION

1 Timothy 4:11-16

This text basically mentions all the scriptures that come to mind, but this lesson is full of revelation...not to plug the book...lol... BUT... this lesson deals with relationship and religion and takes us back to the foundational beginnings of what relationship within religion is supposed to look like. Paul is teaching Timothy, who was afraid to yield to his calling due to his age, how to manage religious relationships despite the date of his birth...Respect is a virtue that transcends every generation and the lessons that he (Paul) is teaching (Timothy and the church) is all about respect. Respect alone will take your ministry further than any good deed. Respect will tear down any wall that you may encounter in your walk with Christ be it in the leader or the follower. Unlike the popular persuasion that is perceived by man, respect can be given for many reasons. Some respect is given because it is inherited with the title that you bear. Some respect is granted for the integrity that you exhibit, and some respect is demanded and granted just for the sake of expectation. When this revelation is received by many men and women of God as well as their followers, I believe that the church will be a better place and the love will be more genuine because the relationships are more genuine.

Day 9

How?

How can a person be spiritually inactive and active at the same time… Many feel that when you are not in church and not doing the "religious thing", as they know it, that you are inactive….for the past few months I have been in a state of discomfort as it relates to the religious sanctity of church, as we know it, and I was crazy enough to ask God why. He revealed to me that in a metamorphosis state during the pupa stage, which is the interim of which a caterpillar becomes a butterfly, no one really knows what is going on inside the cocoon because you can't see it…they are covered right? It's in that covering that the most critical changes take place. See when a caterpillar is born, it is taught to eat all that it can prior to the metamorphosis state because in the cocoon it has to draw from its own self during the pupa phase….the crazy thing that I never thought about is the energy that it takes during the time of inactivity (as it appears)…. ok here is the revelation…we are the caterpillars that are taught to eat all that we can (study to show thyself approved, attending church and the like), then we go through our metamorphosis beginning with the pupa stage wherein, God will remove people from our lives because they are not anointed enough to see God bringing about the change in us, so they cast us away and call us useless. Though they can't see in the cocoon, we can see outside of the cocoon. So we witness the abandonment, and it hurts, but watch this, we are still in the cocoon and let's just be real, it hurts to see people let you down or cast you away…Now watch this…in the cocoon we have to undergo a complete mindset transformation as well as the physical transformation...when we come from our cocoon, we look different, act different, and should be different because of the metamorphosis that has taken place (old things are passed away and behold all things are made new). We should be able to see those people and thank God for them AND their abandonment, because after the relational fatality, focus is restored. Focus brings about the fruition, or the evidence of the change that God has made in us....Our cocoon is our preparation place that God can present us back to the body, after the process, as a purified vessel that God can use despite the bumps and bruises of the past and the abandonment.

CHRISTIAN MONOPOLY

"Christianity is like a game of monopoly, but there is no get out of hell free card, and instead of winning money you win souls."

-Damaria Henderson,
The Anointed Quiet Storm, Minister of Mime

Romans 12:1
*I beseech you therefore, brethren, by the mercies of God, that ye present your bodies a living sacrifice, holy, acceptable unto God, which is your reasonable **service**.*

Many Christians live their lives as if the church of God is a revolving door. They step out and do things that are contrary to their walk and witness and worry more about getting caught by the people of God versus God himself. The thing is you can't hide anything from God because he is everywhere and sees all things, not only as they happen, but before they happen. In order to be rapture ready, we have to remain holy in the midst of it all, even when we see that others are not living out the confessions that they made to Christ. Our ultimate mission is to win souls for Christ. We complete this mission, not so much with the words we say but, with the life that we live. I know there have been several times that I have blown my witness with the words that I said as well as the life that I lived, but I thank God for his grace, mercy and redeeming power. The question is how do you view the lifestyle that you have chosen to live and are you living to the

19

fullest or living it like a fool? The way in which you answer this question should tell you of the work that you have in store. WE must all work out our own soul salvation with fear and trembling and quit gambling with our salvation. Truly no man knows the day nor the hour when the son of man shall appear. As soon as you think of completing an act that is contrary to his will and his way, he may just appear and you will be left behind so just be you and give God a whole hearted "YES" so that he can begin the good work in you, and you won't find yourself trying to bargain your way into heaven.

Day 11

SHOW YOURSELF APPROVED OR PROVE YOURSELF?

2 Timothy 2:15
Study to shew thyself approved unto God, a workman that needeth not to be ashamed, rightly dividing the word of truth.

This is one of the most quoted scriptures by men and women of God to get their members to attend Bible study, Sunday school and other Christian education ventures that many churches lack nowadays. In that form and context this is a super powerful scripture. However, that is not the context that many pastors and preachers apply when they study.

I have had the privilege of sitting amongst some of Christendom's greatest as well as some of its worst. Now please understand that I am not judging, but merely making a point. I have been in awe of some of the leaders I have seen who can speak scripture, saying and citing it, in their mere conversation. I often wonder, "How do they do that?" I have even asked God to give me that gift (for lack of a better term). When I asked him that, the question that he asked me back was, "Will you use it to show yourself approved, or to prove yourself?" I was alarmed when he asked me such a question because I thought that the answer was a no brainer. Before he spoke any more on the matter he heightened my sensitivity to the conversations of those who already possessed the "gift" and the manners in which they use it. I was clearly amazed by what I witnessed. Many leaders use it to prove themselves and create a false sense of value because of their seeming knowledge. I have sat and watched many preachers have

21

a scripture bashing match amongst themselves and even worse in the presence of laypeople or congregants who lack this seeming gift and often walk away confused and many walk away with a made up mind that I won't be back. Even in Bible days when debates broke out amongst the people. They brought the matters to the elders of the church and the elders "behind closed doors" considered it, and came back with a decision on how to handle the matter, they never debated the matter in front of the people (Acts 15). Let us be careful, people of God, not to hurt or hinder the people with our battles to make others believe in us more than they believe in whom we speak of. We have to be careful that we use the gifts that God gives us in the right manner and that we use them to edify the body and glorify God and not ourselves. Beware when people, no matter the title, come to you quoting scriptures, ask God to see beyond their words and into their motives and then make your decision to partake in the conversation or not based on that revelation.

Day 12

I GOT AN "AND" IN MY SPIRIT

1 Peter 5:10
But the God of all grace, who hath called us unto his eternal glory by Christ Jesus, after that ye have suffered a while, make you perfect, stablish, strengthen, settle you.

Have you ever been a place where you have never felt so empty, emotionally unavailable and numb all at the same time? I have. Not only have I felt that way, but I have resided in that place for an extended period of time. I sat around and sung my woe is me song for the longest time and when people tried to get me to talk about it all I could say is, "I can't articulate the magnitude of my pain or even find the words to express my feelings." When I wrote my first book, I had a massive launch wherein I brought people from all over to render in whichever way God saw fit for them to. During that time I had so many "friends" and "supporters" even as I began to speak, I expressed to them that I was in one of the loneliest places of my life and likened it unto a funeral where from the announcement to the funeral so many people are there, but when the ashes hit the dust you are left alone to pick up the pieces on your own. I cried myself to sleep at night, gave up on pursuing my passions and wasted away asking God, "why me?" I was attacked on every side, "friends" left, supporters were few and I had to do a complete replacement of my staff, actually I went back to doing everything myself. One day it all hit me and I couldn't even speak because of the tears that fell. I lost my home, my sanity, my sanctity as well as all desire to fellowship with another. I was as broken as I had ever been. My church had broken apart, which left me broken because it wasn't the first time, and everyone I felt that I could call or count on seemed way too busy for me and I wasn't in a place that I felt that I could be judged or heed to another unkind word or spirit. Finally after months of being in this position, God put an "and" in my spirit that slowly day by day as my strength grew I confessed it every day when something came my way or people failed to find the right words to say, my response was, "and?" Then one day before my eyes got dim I read 1 Peter 5:10 and the first word was, "But." Why is this important? Glad you asked! Both "and" and "but" are conjunctions meaning they are connecting words. What do they connect? It connects my pain to my passion, my destruction to my destiny my past to my present as well as my future. Get a conjunction in your spirit and hang on to it when you have no words to say just give a conjunction and watch the Lord make a way. After that work, whatever your conjunction is you are provoking a turnaround in your situation.

THE QUIET STORM?
HOW CAN HE BE QUIET IN MY STORM

Mark 4:35-41

³⁵And the same day, when the even was come, he saith unto them, Let us pass over unto the other side. ³⁶And when they had sent away the multitude, they took him even as he was in the ship. And there were also with him other little ships. ³⁷And there arose a great storm of wind, and the waves beat into the ship, so that it was now full. ³⁸And he was in the hinder part of the ship, asleep on a pillow: and they awake him, and say unto him, Master, carest thou not that we perish? ³⁹And he arose, and rebuked the wind, and said unto the sea, Peace, be still. And the wind ceased, and there was a great calm. ⁴⁰And he said unto them, Why are ye so fearful? how is it that ye have no faith? ⁴¹And they feared exceedingly, and said one to another, What manner of man is this, that even the wind and the sea obey him?

Many times when we go through the storms of our life, we forget that God will never leave us nor forsake us, especially considering that he rarely speaks in the times of our storms. The reason for this is because he has given us everything that we need to sustain us during that time, but we fail to recognize it until after the storm is over. The saying that hindsight is 20/20 is not a mere cliché, but it is a truth. See if you read the entire chapter 4 of Mark, you will see that the disciples had just witness all of this word taught by Jesus through parables. Common sense would have said that the test was coming since the lesson was over so Jesus went to sleep in full confidence that if nobody grasped the lessons, surely the disciples should have, but still in the midst of the storm they still felt fearful.

My friends, I tell this to you as a word of encouragement that if Jesus was there with them in the flesh and they panicked and failed the test, then surely since we cannot see him in the flesh we will encounter the same periods of unbelief. The encouraging part is that if we only seek him for a mere "one word" it will turn your complete situation around. Question is will you seek him during the time of your test or will you sit beside him and worry?

WHEN YOU LEAST EXPECT IT!

John Chapter 5

What I love about God is that he will do an extraordinary thing at an unorthodox time. See men have a time and a season in which they believe that a thing should happen, but the scripture clearly states that his ways are higher than our ways and his thoughts are higher than ours (Isaiah 55:9) so this means that God will do what he wants, when he wants and even greater, HOW he wants. It's all about being in the right place at the right time. This man was sitting at the pool waiting for 2 things which are common components that many of us wait upon in times of crisis and those two components are people and time. The fatality in his waiting is that both components can and often times will work against you. He said to Jesus, that he was waiting for the troubling of the water (time/circumstance) and then he said he was waiting for someone to help him in the pool when the time comes. He went on to say that when he "tries" another person steps before him.

Lesson here is that man will fail you and time is not on your side. But be encouraged my brothers and sisters, why fret over the foolishness of these components when the creator of both elements is standing there waiting to attend to your needs, all you have to do is position yourself in the right place at the right time which is in the perfect will of God.

Many of us pursue the symptoms of the gift and have a tendency of overlooking the source and gift giver. Please understand that God has to first reveal these truths to me before I can reveal them to you so these truths are hitting me as the writer before it hits you. So I echo the words of Apostle Paul, "I count not myself to have apprehended...." We are learning together!

Day 15

It's Critical I Don't Return

John 5:14

Afterward Jesus findeth him in the temple, and said unto him, Behold, thou art made whole: sin no more, lest a worse thing come unto thee.

When we experience the healing of Christ we have to walk in the assurance that it is done. For this man, this was a literal revelation. See after Christ had healed him, man tried to say things to him to distract his celebration. When he returned to the temple to see who it was who had healed him, he found Jesus and was able to put a name to the voice that commanded him to do such an unorthodox act. The revelation here is that we cannot allow man to kill the clemency that was awarded to us by the father. To do such a thing is an insult to God.

I am reminded of a time when I was a teacher in a preschool and a parent had come and asked me could she give her child a party in my class. I granted her the permission to do so only for the time to arrive and the guests to be in place and the child to look at his mom upon her surprise for him and told her that it wasn't his birthday. The mother looked at him and said, I know, I did it only because I love you! My point to you is God does not need a designated day to do what it is that you need but he will do it in his time and in his way.

TEMPERATURE CHECK

Daniel 3:19

Then was Nebuchadnezzar full of fury, and the form of his visage was changed against Shadrach, Meshach, and Abednego: therefore he spake, and commanded that they should heat the furnace one seven times more than it was won't to be heated.

The greatest understanding that one can have is the revelation that when God is getting ready to bless you and take you to a greater dimension in him, the devil recognizes it and is not going to let you get elevated that easy. He is going to crank up his strategy to keep you discouraged and in a defeated mindset so that it will be manifested in your actions through adverse emotional actions such as depression, anger, resentment, doubt, and even suicide. The higher the level, the hotter the heat. Many of us look at the achievement and accolades of others and we want to have what they have and be where they are without knowing the behind the scenes effort that it took to get them to that point. I remember when I was touring with some gospel artists and I was assisting in the preparation for their tour and I always thought that touring was just showing up to sing your song and keep it moving, but to my surprise there are thousands of hours that go into the efforts of planning before the production. So it is in your spiritual walk, it takes lots of heat to purify you for usage in the kingdom. Just remember that when you go through the fire, not only does God promise to take you higher, but he will also be there with you as well.

THE PROTECTED WANDERER
"THE CRUTCH OF CAIN"

2 Chronicles 7:14

If my people, which are called by my name, shall humble themselves, and pray, and seek my face, and turn from their wicked ways; then will I hear from heaven, and will forgive their sin, and will heal their land.

When Cain killed Abel, he was sure that the people would put a hit out on him and try to take his life, but God in his sovereign love encouraged Cain, even in his messed-up state, that he would charge anyone who did him harm seven times the usual punishment of normalcy. In this way God protected Cain and gave him a chance to see the error of his ways and to repent to get it right.

Even in the midst of your personal chaos and confusion God will still cover you while you're in your muck and mire and he will still put a charge on your head for any harm that may come to your dwelling. This is done as an effort to give you a chance to get it right. See only Church folk automatically condemn you to hell at the first sight of a mistake, but the God of all grace will give you a chance to get it right before he turns you over to the reprobate state. Reprobate is defined as a depraved, unprincipled or wicked person or a person rejected by God and beyond hope of salvation. No one really wants to find themselves in this condition. It is a shame to live your whole life to go to heaven to allow one mistake or setback to send you to hell. Take this opportunity to repent and turn from your wicked ways and start again!

Repent in its purest form is "re" and "pent." Re- means again or again and again in a repetitious manner. –Pent means shut in or confined. When you put these two words together you will see that God wants you to repent meaning to come under his covering once again and stay there. To die to our flesh daily means that we understand that we are and forever will be a work in progress and will never get it perfectly right because, no good thing dwells in this flesh that we live in.

He Wants You and All That is Connected to You, Everyone in Your Class and Category

Matthew 2:16

Then Herod, when he saw that he was mocked of the wise men, was exceeding wroth, and sent forth, and slew all the children that were in Bethlehem, and in all the coasts thereof, from two years old and under, according to the time which he had diligently inquired of the wise men.

When God has something in store for you, no devil in hell can keep it from you. See the devil only sees you as a potential threat, he doesn't really have a true revelation of who you are and the truth is neither do you. The Bible proves this when it says, "eyes have not seen, ears have not heard, neither has it entered into the heart of man, the things that God has in store for you. So in his ignorant rage the enemy tries to find where you are and when your protective angels outwit him then not only does he go after you but everyone and everything connected to you. And everyone like your kind. This tells us of the importance of teams and/or connections. See you have to watch who you are connected to because in an effort to get to you, he will attack those that are close to you, especially if you are empowering their spirit and their anointing is charged and ignited by your anointing so please beware!

Many times we find ourselves associated with people for various reasons and they are connected to us for several reasons. The catch is to find those reasons and make sure that they are pure and right. Abraham and Lot were associated first and foremost because they were related, but if you read the story in its entirety you will see that Abraham could not receive his promise until he separated from Lot and when the separation took place, Abraham gave Lot whatever it was that he wanted and Lot took the best that Abraham had. Of course this was paining Abraham's humanity but when he released his best God granted him even better than the best that he had and he also gave him more than what he had to begin with. Watch you connections!

Day 19

BE SET TO BESET

Hebrews 12:1 (Whole Chapter)

Wherefore seeing we also are compassed about with so great a cloud of witnesses, let us lay aside every weight, and the sin which doth so easily beset us, and let us run with patience the race that is set before us,

The hardest part about the transition that we make when we give our lives to Christ is the changes that we have to make. The detriment that makes it hard is when people see the changes that we have to make for the sake of the Kingdom. The cloud of witnesses that this passage speaks of, are the people who see the transformation that God makes in you right before their eyes. He understands that they will all have their opinions and perceptions of what you should do and how you should do it so God goes ahead and lets you know not to pay it any attention but to lay aside the weight of their opinion because judgment is a sin and if you allow, their opinions will beset you from how Christ has anointed you to be set. We will be set free when we see that often times people judge what they don't understand and especially if it is outside the box of their normalcy. I remember in my comedy act as, "Jennifiyah" the Christian comedienne, I poked fun at the women of holiness who banned makeup because of the fact that they saw people who didn't know how to apply it and so they figured if it looked that bad then it had to be a sin. This is what the Bible means when it talks about modest apparel, which means do not cake the makeup on, but merely cover the imperfections. I am laughing out loud but it is true, I am so interested to see what we see when we get to heaven. I am sure that we will see some of the things that we as believers have condemned to hell, like some forms of gospel music and the like, but the point of the matter is that we cannot be moved by people's opinions and perceptions and we have to move with the cloud of glory and not the crowd of people.

SINGLE AND SETTLING

Just because you are single does not mean that you have to settle. I have seen many people run away from singleness and honestly I have done so myself for many years. But when I became a woman, a professional, mature in the faith, I put away childish things. I realized that there was more to me than being the trophy on someone else's arm. I realize that Christ is all of the validation that I need. Many of us get into relationships because we are looking to be validated and honestly a relationship is not what does the trick. Looking into the word of God and seeing what he says about you is more validation than one can stand. The need for validation is a type of illness that no one can medicate, but it causes for deliverance. Deliverance from all symptoms that are attached to it such as low self-esteem, self-pity, depression, anger, anxiety of being alone, a needy mentality, just to name a few. Everyone talks about meeting their Boaz, but if that be the case, then that means you have to play the part of Ruth and be about your business and make sure that when you come to the table that you have your own, hold your own and own your own, that lets the other individual know that clearly you are an asset and not a liability, a pro not a con, a plus and not a minus, you get the picture. Over the years, I have had men call me an overachiever, arrogant, crazy, doing too much and the list goes on, and for a long time I believed them, but God never let me lose my drive to achieve my dreams of being highly educated, an entrepreneur, a business woman in every aspect of the word and in street terms a hustler. I have two children to feed and I had been doing it alone for 19 and 21 years, I want to be the example that I want them to look for in a mate. I need my son to know what a virtuous woman looks like so that he doesn't fall victim to the Delilah or Jezebel spirit, and I want my daughter to see what she needs to do to make herself above the common. I challenge you today to do the same because even if you're tired at the end of the day, you can look in the mirror and say, "I DID THAT!" #What a great feeling!

BETWEEN JUDAS AND JOHN

If you allow your encounter with Judas to get you down and kill your spirit to pursue your purpose, you will never encounter your John. When Jesus sat at the table for the Last Supper, I believe prophetically he was strategically placed between John, the forerunner for his ministry and Judas, the betrayer. This is critical because, if truth be told, there are more Judas' in our life than there are Johns. Be not dismayed because you can't have one without the other. When you encounter the Judas' in your life you have to understand that they are vital to your success. You have a choice to decide whether they are going to make you better or bitter. To become bitter only procrastinates the expected end that Christ has for you and impedes the process that you have to partake in to pursue your purpose. To be better means that you understand that you can take the betrayal of Judas and make it into the pin that punctures the sack and pushes you into labor forcing you to deliver the baby that is destined to come as a result of the persecution. Remember when Jesus was talking to the disciples in Mark about the promises that he made to them to give them 100 fold of all that they sacrificed, he assured them that it would come, but not without persecution. Many of us quote the famous, "the last will be first, and the first will be last" but we fail to see the revelation in that statement which means that your persecutions will push you back. As it tries to push you to throw in the towel, but the more that you persevere through the adversity, the more muscles that you will gain. Remember this, a plane always flies against the wind because it is the opposition that makes it rise to the sky and soar above the current situation. If a plane is already in the air and it starts to rain, it just rises above the cloud, but if it hasn't taken off then the flight is often delayed until the weather clears. Get in the air and weather the storm!

THE VERBS OF CHRISTENDOM

What is a verb? A verb is an action word. Everywhere He went He was doing good".... He was moved with compassion and He did this and that"..... "He taught them" ... "He loved us"..... THESE ARE ALL ACTIONS.... We can talk, talk, talk, and continue trying to impress one or many, but that is all it will be, "just talk and meaningless words" We can pray, pray, pray, "faith without works is dead" show me your action and I will tell you of your belief/faith .... We can speak in tongues day and night nonstop, that tongues' speaking is for your edification, the question then will be, "How edified are you at the end of your tongues speaking? "Jesus was not just saying good everywhere He went, He was also doing good, living good, His life was about His words, they were in unison He and His words. Then the Apostles continued in unison with the words and teachings of God, they turned the cities upside down with their different words and lifestyle, hence the reason they were called "CHRISTIANS" of which this name is being abused today. Don't just talk about it, be about it! Just do what it is that thus saith the Lord and watch him work it to your benefit as well as the benefit of others.

Day 23

You Can Sit at the Table with Me

Because God is love, he has selected some of the worst to be made the best. He has taken worthless matter and transformed it into pure gold. God's love purchased lives to set apart the worst of mankind to be the reward of the Savior's ardor. The powerful grace of God calls some of the most disgraceful to sit at the table of mercy and none of them to remain hopeless, but rising full of hope in Him. Never look to someone else and just assume that because of their past, you have a better chance at salvation. God's saving grace is for those who trust and believe in Him, for those who will stand on his everlasting word, those who in the midst of trial, stand with non-wavering faith, knowing that God is God and even when we don't see the outcome looking promising, we know that he is already victorious and so shall we be just that victorious and he shall in all things get the glory... father I pray that my life and all I do bring glory unto your name.

Trust your soul with God and He will bring you to that place where you will sit at the table with Him. Don't read the Word or hear the Word and turn away as though life and death mean nothing because as sure as there is heaven, there is hell and they are both going to be occupied!

Day 24

STOLEN OR GIVEN

At times I am amazed at the words of people, especially church folks, we talk so much and it is just words...

We talk about ALLLLLL that the devil "stole" from us and how we will take it back, the thing is that we look at the devil taking it and then we want to go and take it back, then the taking back is in words only. We talk about the enemy is keeping us from possessing our land when we stand/sit there doing nothing about possessing our land. We talk about how we will have what God said we will have, then we see one sign of opposition, and we are ready to run away and oftentimes, do run, let us look through the word of God, there was always a fight for what God gave His people, because we have an enemy (Adversary). We talk about the enemy will not prevent us from having what God is going to give us, however we are not standing in line with God's words for us to have the said thing. My question for you is this, did the enemy steal your promise or did you give it away? I know it sounds ludicrous to think that we give away our God given promise but we do with our lives that are contrary to the will of God and the choices that we make that are in the way of the deliverance of our promises. Many speak peace and then entangle with forms of bondage that become terroristic threats to the peace God gives. Did the enemy take it or did you give it to him?

Day 25

CATCH UP

When you've wasted a lot of precious time with the wrong people and doing the wrong thing, you have to make that time up. Because of Jonah's initial rebellion; he was still required to make the three day's journey to Nineveh to preach repentance before the destined and appointed time of God's wrath was to hit the city. Listen, God doesn't change His mind just because we are out of place. We had better change our minds to coincide with His. Jonah had to make up the lost time and so do we. We must run, not walk, to catch up with what Heaven is doing. Elijah was in such a hurry, he outran the chariot! Imagine that, running faster than a car trying to accomplish the will of God!! Lord, help us and please help me!! Open my blind eyes so I won't waste any more time on foolery!! The next time the enemy sends a minute matter your way just remind him, you have delayed me long enough, now I am catching up to my promise. When they lie on you, say I'm catching up to my promise. When they talk about you tell them, I'm catching up to my promise. Don't let anyone or anything else deter you, tell them I'M CATCHING UP TO MY PROMISE!

WORSHIP

Let's look at the word "worship"
Worship is actually a compound word
"wor"-short for worth….Ship (as a suffix) is defined as

1 denoting a quality or condition: companionship | friendship.
2 denoting status, office, or honor: ambassadorship | citizenship..
   denoting a tenure of office : chairmanship.
3 denoting a skill in a certain capacity: entrepreneurship.
4 denoting the collective individuals of a group: membership.

This means that your service in worship should not only reflect how much God means to you but also how much the calling means to you. How much you value a person is denoted in your service to them. Contrary to popular demand, ministry is more about serving than it is about the man or the limelight, but all about the ability to serve. We are all called to be a servant both vertically and horizontally. So worship the Lord in spirit and in truth and let him know just how much he means to you!

JUST BE REAL

Let us be very careful of being church goers in the house of God. It is time to stop the church act/church going, and time to be real in Jesus name. Dearly beloved brethren, I write this to you in all the love I have for you from my father which is in heaven, Let us be very careful of being church goers in the house of God, it makes no sense that we just go to church and are not living the life that God calls us to live, that will be fooling our own selves, the word of God said that "by our fruit people will know who we are", I ask you what fruit are you displaying both in your words and your actions? God never ask for us to go to church, dance, skip, shout and speak in tongues so that people will know we are his children, He said by our love first to Him, then to one another in thoughts, words, and action, they will know that we are His children. Not by gossiping about each other, (gossipers will not inherit the kingdom of God), not by betraying each other's confidence, (thus causing strife), not by telling lies to and about each other (God hates lies), not by spreading rumors and slandering each other's names (God hates malice), not by carrying news to leadership about each other, (looking for man's reward). Love is love, God is love and He displayed that in action by sending His only son to die for us all, all of us were wretched sinners and yet he still loved us, He never treated us bad in spite of what we have done and what we are still doing today in our frail human state, neither will He allow us to get in a corner and speak ill of one another and get away with it. The days for fooling ourselves in church is over, I have been there and done that, it is time for us to come from off that junction, and choose our road. In choosing our road, we may have to choose different friends, but that's alright God can give us friends after His own heart, friends that will help us to make it in with Him. It is time to stop the church act. It is said if one wants to see the real Hollywood, go in churches, that statement needs to be changed, but sad to say it is correct to a point, because I myself don't understand how it is, that we can go to church speak in tongues and yet deal treacherously with one another, that is acting in tongue, not the Holy Ghost in operation. Let us be careful because there is a spirit called a "religious spirit" it will fall on us, so be very careful in Jesus name lest we become possessed with this evil spirit, it knows the scriptures, knows the word, knows the truth, knows how to pray, worship, and every other religious activity in the church, yet fail to do the right things and behave as though the wrong things that are being done is the right thing. God forbid! Church is not going to save anyone of us, it is only the beginning of our spiritual journey, the entrance gate to our everlasting kingdom, it is time to get out the entrance and dwell in the kingdom, the very secret place of the most High. I have seen the spirit of anger as a terrifying monster raise its head in the church, I have seen people behave with actions of pure hate, I have seen people telling lies on one another with tears in their eyes, I have seen leaders hugging devils and kicking saints, I have never seen that in the world from which I came. The church has too many hurting people and pains, not forgetting shame, let us search ourselves individually, and work out our own soul salvation with Godly fear and reverence. Let us practice to do the right things and associate with the right people so that we will make heaven our home and rest in the mansions that is already prepared for us.

Day 28

ROOTED OR ROTTED

When a plant grows the first thing that has to be established is the root. If there is no root established, the plant may still grow but it will rot and be moved at the first sign of adverse conditions, extended exposure to sunlight, wind, excessive rain, storms and the like. So it is with us as Christians. When we seek to have a relationship with the Lord we need to establish a relationship that is rooted in the word of God which will sustain us through storm and rain. Many of us attend church, Bible study, conferences and other Christian events and never intake the word and meditate on it to allow it to establish root in our spirits that the word will be made manifest in our actions. Examine yourself to see if you are rotten or rooted in the word. How do you know the difference? I am glad you asked! Look at the lifestyle that you lead. Ask yourself, "does the life that I live speak of Christ and all he has done for me? Does the way that I carry myself speak of the salvation that I have experienced and the redemption that I have received as a result thereof? When people see me, do they encounter the Christ that is in me or the chaos that is in me?" If that self-examination doesn't work, then look at the people who surround you, watch their actions, their words, their conversation, their lifestyle. Many try to discredit the guilty by association theory, but in reality it is a truth that needs to be exposed and revealed. It is not very often, if at all, do you find several types of birds associated and accumulated in one area together, yet you see them of a like kind flocking together. Thus the cliché, "birds of a feather, flock together." Who you flocking with is a clear reflection of who you are.

A SEED

A seed is an end result in disguise that if properly nurtured and cared for can end in the desired result of its purpose. The word of God is a seed that is planted in our hearts in hopes that it will be planted, nurtured and cared for in a manner that will be conducive to the expected end that Christ has for us, our destiny. Many people plant a seed and keep a watch on it as their expected end is made manifest. This is what concerns me about Church goers because they are said to be "seeded" but nothing is being manifested. This is why our walk is so critical because it is the exemplification of what we have planted. You can't plant the word of God in your heart and raise hell? That is the same as planting an apple seed and receiving a pecan tree. Ludicrous! (In the words of Mike Tyson…lol). When we are evangelizing others we have to be mindful of the seeds that we plant in others because that seed will be manifested and the responsibility will lie on your shoulders. Don't let anyone threaten your seed, protect it with your very life and hold on to the hope and expectation of greatness. Plant your seed and give it room to grow but remember that it takes time and energy to produce the expected end which means it needs a lot of SONlight, pruning, purging, and nurturing.

GIVE IT ROOM TO GROW

When you plant a seed in the life of someone else, back up and give it room to grow! Sometimes, we as leaders are guilty of trying to play God and feel obligated to the process of planting, plucking, watering, pruning and making growth happen. It is a great effort if the motive is right, but honestly this is not what God called us to do. Jesus called, appointed and then anointed the disciples before he sent them out. We have to remember that we are not Christ and that the charge that we have is to extend and it is for the people to accept or reject. We are to set up the edifice and curriculum in which we take advantage of teachable moments for Kingdom sake and then we step back and watch the word do the work in the lives of the people. When we hover over plants all of the time and continuously feed and water them without exposing them to sunlight, we are going to kill them, but it's when we step back and allow the seed to be exposed to sunlight that growth takes place. If we expose the people whom God has given us charge over to the SONlight, then he will make sure that increase happens and we can move on to next plant or maybe even the harvest. Remember everything that we do is about time and season and as long as the season and the time interact with each other then it will be easier for us to gauge our purpose in the life of the individuals and we will know our responsibility, but just always remember to step back and give it room to grow.

Day 31

THE LOVE OF THE SEED IN ME

If you love the seed in me, then you can handle the fruit of me. Many people love where I am now, wherever that is, but I have also had a level of resistance in my life in reference to relationships because they didn't understand that I was nurturing the seed that was placed in me, but when the fruits of that labor began to be manifested people came out of the wood works to taste of the fruit. I dare you today to allow God to place people who love the seed that comes before the fruit in your life. Many marriages fail because they can't handle the planting of the seed and the nurturing that has to take place to include the pruning that is detrimental to the growth process. Every beautiful thing that you experience started off as a seed. Seeds come in many form; words, deeds, observations and even inheritance. Seeds are the beginning thing of a beautiful end. I have always shared my inability to garden or grow flowers because I want to see the end result. When I was married before I used to always watch my father in law "play in his grass" and talk to it and be ever so attentive to it. For years, we thought that he was "doing too much" and that he looked crazy outside talking to, nurturing, and cultivating his grass, but at the end of the day he always had the greenest grass and the greatest lawn. We never knew that it was preparation for his future calling as a Pastor of a church where he later took that same amount of time and patience with the souls that he was entrusted with. Why? Because he knew he had to give them time to grow.

THE PIT AND THE PALACE

Many times people lose their hope when they find themselves in a less than comfortable place. Everyone shouts when the flowers are blooming and the sun is shining, but as soon as the chips are down and circumstances are less than favorable we blame the enemy when oftentimes; it is God setting us up for elevation in the form of pruning us of excess weight. But remember if you can prosper in the pit and the prison you can prosper in the palace. What does this mean? Paul said it best when he said I know what it is to be abased and abound and in whatever state that I am in I am content. The revelation of this is that you cannot lose hope when obstacles come your way. We have to understand that obstacles are used as stepping stones when perceived correctly. Opposition is only what we make it, we can choose to look at it as opposition against us, or an opportunity to see God arrange them to work FOR us. When we learn to celebrate his glory in the plot of the story, then we have shown him that we can be trusted in whatever state that we find ourselves in remembering that all things really do work together for our good and no weapon formed against us shall prosper and every tongue that rise against us (that tries to kick us while we are down) will have to fall (come back and eat the same words that they spoke against us) and find themselves needing the testimony that we have of how we overcame to assist them in their own walk! Many times it is the people that spoke less than favorable of us that need us in the long run. Whatever you do, no matter how you feel, just be assured and remember it is all for his glory and your story.

Day 33

What is Holiness?

Holiness is not in my dress outside, but the condition of my inside. Holiness has become an extinct characteristic or personification of what we thought was to serve as a witness to a religious experience. In reality, holiness is a lifestyle. It is the condition to hang on to God and his expectation come what may. When many people think of holiness they think of the religious spirit that is in church and is inherited or granted on people after they have been laboring for hours in and out of "the spirit" and who seem to pray til Jesus shows up and even if he delays, they continue to pray. These people go to church several times out of the week and wear dresses to their toenails and have a subservient attitude in regards to life. Well my friend, please allow me to be the one to tell you that even having all of these characteristics you can still have a lifestyle that does not exude any form of holiness, let alone Godliness. Stop entertaining the world's interpretation of Holiness and get in hot pursuit of God's righteousness and order, and it is a guarantee that living will be a whole lot easier. There are people who show us a form of Godliness and speak to our "religious expectation" that our experience in the days of old have taught us what holiness looks like. Do you remember when the mothers of the church said, "You can't wear red polish because it was for harlots?" Or how about, "If your skirt came above your knees, you were advertising yourself to the men of the church?" Let's not even get into their expectations of us as women being professional and working outside of the home. For the longest time I was disturbed by these beliefs until I educated myself with knowledge and began to look at the root of these beliefs, after which holiness took on a whole different form for me. Holiness, to me, is living in the authenticity of the truth that is YOU! Realize that it is all about the relationship that you have with Christ and his expectation of you as an individual. Embodying this truth is authenticated when you do a thing and you are convicted about it, not because of what others say and do, and surely not because of their beliefs. Ask God today "What does your holiness look like?"

I UNDERSTAND NOW

As a girl being abused and misused, I was left thinking that the world was against me and that no one loved me. I thought my mother hated me and my father took the first opportunity to leave me when he and my mother fell out. I felt that my brother despised me and never regarded me as the loving sister that I tried so hard to be. It took many years for me to see that these individuals as well as the others who have come in and out of my life only did what they knew how. They showed me love as they experienced it. Many times we expect more from people than they are actually able to accommodate. It allowed me to see how God feels when we love him to get what we want and then forget about him when we get it. Many times when we go through things, we get angry and lash out at God because we don't understand it, but the time has come and now is for us to understand that it is all by design. No inventor ever releases an invention without testing it out first, so this test was given to us by design because we are made in his image and shapened in his likeness, but we have to go through the test before we can be released. Come on and tell your neighbor, I UNDERSTAND NOW! Many times we try to see people for how they are now and just charge it to their character without investing the time and energy to get to know them and understand the "why" behind the "how" they do things. Especially when it comes to the relationships that we enter into, "understanding" comes in many forms and must be apprehended before the love and the relationship can be appreciated.

MANIPULATORS BY NATURE

There have been times in my life that I have forfeit who I was so that I could fit in with others when clearly that is not what or who I was called to be, but because the enemy is a master manipulator he would make me think that I was missing something and that the grass is greener on the other side. How many of us have lost something because we thought that the grass was greener on the other side. Not only will the enemy manipulate you, but he will also use people to manipulate you. We are all manipulators by nature and the crazy thing is that we don't have to learn to be that way, we are born that way. As an infant our first understanding is that if we want something, and since we don't have the vocabulary to attain it, we just cry and someone will come running. This manipulative behavior comes because we understand the association of cause and effect. We carry this innate trait with us for life and it is up to us as to how we use it. The Bible says that we are to compel people to come. It does not mean manipulate people to come to Christ and then coerce them to think like you and adopt your ways or behaviors. In relationships, people learn what the other person likes or doesn't like and we use that to get what we want from them. Manipulation! As a teacher, I make learning fun as a manner of manipulation to get the students to catch the concept that I am teaching. Go ahead and embrace the fact that we are manipulators by nature, but use your inheritance to gain your Godly inheritance and not manipulation.

IT'S OKAY THAT I AM NOT LIKE YOU

Many times in life I always felt like I was less than. Truth is even after I came to know Christ and I was even operating in ministry, I still had an inferiority complex because I knew that I was different. I thought different, I spoke different, I do right because I want to, not because I have to. I am a creature of habit so therefore I love structure and routine. Every now and again I will bust of out that shell, but for the most part, I am pretty predictable as far as routines, processes and procedures. The truth of that matter is that many of us don't take the time to have intimacy (INTO ME SEE) with God so that he can show us ourselves and can exemplify the manner in which he made us and why. It seems as though it is taking forever, but I am still learning to be okay with being different. I am doing my best not to let people really get under my skin when they ridicule me for not being like them. I embrace the fact that one degree may be good enough for you, but I wanted more. Writing a single book may be one person's dream, but mine was that I wanted to write a book every year for the rest of my life, after I published my first one. I am unlike anyone else because I know that I am called to be different and NOW I AM learning to be OKAY WITH IT! As I grow into this truth the more free that I become and the more liberated I am to operate in my truth and execute God's desire for my life as authentically as possible. Did you ever think of how insulting to God it must be when we do not embrace who he created us to be? Think about that for a second. For those who have children, how would you feel if they came to you and said I hate you for having me and making me look like this? My hair is short and straight and I want it I long and curly. Even worse for those with a mate if your mate who once loved and adored you came and said, "I hate I married you because you are built like this!" when you were the same size the day you met. Such insult is what God feels when we try to pattern ourselves after others because he, himself designed us with purpose and destiny in mind.

THE ULTIMATE DESIGNER

Many of us go through things in life and are ready to throw in the towel and are fearful of our ability to handle the adversity that is life. When we are Christians, we are expected to have a strong facade that says that, "I have it all together." While we all recognize the scripture that says, "I am fearfully and wonderfully made", many of us don't get the revelation therein. We were made by the ultimate designer. The one who created us in his image and likeness built us for the life that we live. Am I saying that every day is going to be perfect? No, but what I am saying is that you are a designers original and no one can do you or be you like you can so hold your head back, stick your chest out and walk it out. I am reminded of the times that my children would always say, "Mommy, I want to be just like you when I get big!" I remember seeing the love and adoration in their eyes for me and then they got older. By the time they were older I had a number of degrees and host of other things going on in my life and I did it all being a single parent with two children, one of which had special needs. When my daughter had my grandson, I remember hearing her cry in bed at night and face the frustration of trying to walk in my shoes by trying to go to school, work full time, and raise a baby. In her eyes she failed because she was not able to keep it all together, but in my eyes she was the ultimate success story when she realized she couldn't do as I had done and began finding and living in her own skin and not trying to be like mom. Trying to be someone else or do what others do is an impossible task. I realize now that when you are anointed and appointed to do a thing to others you

73

make it look easy and then when they try to do it they experience the epic failure. It is our job as motivators to remind others that though I am sent to motivate you, I am not motivating you to make you a mini me, but I am motivating you to live in your authentic skin and embrace the design in which you were created.

Day 38

TAKE THAT BUT LEAVE MY PEACE!

As much as we may want to live in the lullaby spa atmosphere of peace, life happens. When life happens there are certain things that rock us to the core and have a tendency to rob us of our peace. Bills, finances, family, relationships, children, jobs, responsibility; all of these things have a connection to us that if we allow it, will rob us of our peace. We must mature to a point that we allow the enemy to touch what he wants, take what he wants, but we still reside in that place of peace that passeth all understanding. This place of maturity says, "You can have it all, but just leave my peace." I remember each time I went through a divorce as the primary breadwinner in the relationships it seemed as though I would always come up with the short end of the stick, but I matured to a place that says, "You can have it all, but just leave my peace." I have had jobs, at which I made a lot of money, but the stress levels were super high and it began to affect my health but I chose to let them go and say, "you can have it all, but just leave my peace." I used to let the issues that my children encountered affect me and I would always take their issues personally until finally I found the place that said, "You can have it all, but just leave my peace." My charge to you is to find that place in your life that says, "You can have it all, but just leave my peace," and stay there.

BRACE YOURSELF, GOD IS ABOUT TO HIT THE GAS!

Many of us have been waiting on something in particular from God. This thing is something that it takes others years to get, but I tell you now to brace yourself for what God is getting ready to do. It's a supernatural acceleration of time. It's the last will be first and the first will be last type of exchange. It's that be last type of blessing that says, "I may not be first in line, but as long as I finished there is a greater reward in it for me!" It's that desire of your heart type manifestation that makes your breathing become deeper and your heart to begin racing because there is an expectancy in your spirit that says, "Oh yes, it is my time and my turn!" I'm not T.D. Jakes but I do feel that famous, "Get Ready, Get Ready, Get Ready" in my spirit. Get your house in order today. You've been praying the prayer of Jabez long enough, now live it, do it, be it, and walk it out.

WHEN MY SENSES ARE LYING TO ME!

We have all been taught to trust our senses. See, touch, taste, hear and smell, but how many times have we allowed our emotion and senses to cheat us out of our blessing? I believe God for financial increase, BUT I DON'T SEE AN INCREASE IN MY FUNDS? I want an authentic God-Ordained relationship, YET WE TOUCH WHAT DOESN'T BELONG TO US? Oh taste and see that the Lord is good, BUT I DON'T FEEL HIS PRESENCE IN MY CURRENT SITUATION? What do you say when your senses are lying to you? The Bible says that faith is the substance of things hoped for and the evidence of things not seen. BELIEVE God instead of beating yourself up, trust him when you can't trace him, hear him with your heart; taste him with the deepest yearning in your place of worship. He's there I promise you; just don't be deceived by your humanity (senses).

Day 41

THE BLIND LEADING THE BLIND

Many times, sadly enough, we are finding leaders who are untaught and unlearned leading a people with the same characteristics. This is a combustible situation that can lead to destruction. It is great to have the anointing, but you can't use that as a reason and rationale when talking to unbelievers, you need clarity in your credentials and I am not talking about just book knowledge, but life application knowledge. Learn all you can and apply all you can stand to win over every man to desire to see Jesus Christ in the end. There is nothing more detrimental than an unlearned leader trying to lead an unlearned convert. This is the revelation of the Bible scripture that reads, "Study to show thyself approved a workman that need not be ashamed, RIGHTLY dividing the Word of truth.

Day 42

IT'S NOT THE DESIGN OF MY CLOTHES IT'S THE DESIGNER OF MY BEING THAT MAKES THE DIFFERENCE

We all know people who are materialistic and in need of validation through material things. With that being said, we have to ensure that we don't fall into the traps of the Christian fashion show that takes place in many churches across the world. Many people don't think about the impact that they are having on people who are less fortunate that simply want a word of hope and encouragement and not to feel ostracized by the garments that they wear. Please be advised that the enemy is using all sorts of tactics to divide the church and one of the oldest tricks in the book is the trick of making people feel inferior for whatever reason, be it their clothes, income, social status, sexual orientation, and the like. Let us who know better, help them to mature to a point as we should have already matured to say, "It's not in that other superficial stuff but about the designer of my being that created everything in us that really matters."

I KNOW WHO I AM AND WHOSE I AM AND IT'S NOT THAT!

Many of us go through identity crisis at various points in our lives and sadly enough during those transitions in life we are all convinced that we know who we are. The truth of the matter is that we never really know who or what we are until we seek the face of the master who designed and created us. One thing that is for sure is that though we may never fully grow the fullness of who we are, the reality that we do grasp is the ability to say, "I am NOT that!" As parents, we all feel that we know our children very well and so when we receive reports of things that they are supposed to have done, as a parent we know and state, "My child may do a lot of things, but I know they won't do that!" My question is what is your "that." As a Christian, I have fell into some riotous living situations as did the prodigal son and for the longest time, many would still call me by what I was delivered from and as I matured in life and in Christ, I became bold enough to say to them, "I know who I am and it's not that. Stand firm in your "not that" conviction and be careful not only to ignore the things that people call you, but also what you call yourself for life and death is carried around in your tongue.

THE POWER OF THE NEW PERSPECTIVE

Many of us have a tendency of complaining about the things that we don't have or we show discontent for the things that we do have. My mother used to tell my brother and I that she was damned if she did and damned if she didn't and often times I feel as though God feels the same way. I will never complain again about what I don't have because often there is a blessing in what you don't have. I don't have a husband which means I don't have to worry about having someone abusing and using me for being who I am. I don't have a huge house which means I don't have to worry about living beyond my means and having a mortgage I can't afford. I don't have millions of dollars (YET) which means I don't have to worry about various beggars befriending me because of my wealth. I could go on and on but I think you get my drift, stop counting what you don't have and count the blessing of what that lack means. With that being said, we also have to be careful about complaining about the blessings that we do have the liberty to have. We may not have the six figure job, but we do have a job while many are still unemployed. The word of the day is #newperspective

KINGDOM CONNECTION

Elizabeth and Mary were divinely connected in a manner that only God could orchestrate. There is a saying that people are in your life for one of three reasons; a reason, a season and a lifetime. The interesting part of the puzzle is figuring out why they are there and then handling them accordingly. Abandonment is one of the worst forms of abuse and the reason why is because many people abandon us without reason or at least they don't tell us what the reason is. Spouses may cheat and abandon the household, as the victimized spouse, and even more so, the children of the abandonment, they walk through life with a burning question that asks, "Why?" When we grasp the concept of the triad as to why people enter into our lives, we are able to alleviate those questions and continue on with life believing that though I may not know why they left or what the purpose of our encounter was, I know that it will be revealed by and by. Holding on to the question is a form of self-abuse because it creates the inability for us to move on and enjoy life knowing that our destiny is not tied to them, but to the encounter in which we had. I definitely had to quickly grasp this concept, especially as a single woman who was in the dating scene. I would find myself heartbroken when I thought that this one was "the one" only to find out he wasn't. What I learned is that with each date and each heartbreak, I became more equipped for the single life, and I also became more keen to the games that people ran when their intentions were less than pure. Yes, people come into our lives for a reason, season, or a lifetime, but what they all have in common is the fact that it is all about kingdom connections for the betterment of the individuals involved.

THE SHIFT OF THE ATMOSPHERE

The wise men were anonymously chosen to destroy the destiny of Christ, but chose not to. God will deal with not only you, but the ones that are around you as well. Joseph was careful not to taint Mary her while she carried the promise. The star was the shift in the atmosphere that made the wise men seek to go and see the king and caused a divine disruption in their destinies. There are events and occurrences in our lives that change the very element of our being and serve as a catalyst to change our existence as well as the manner in which we handle things that occur later in our lives and it will also bring clarity to some prior situations. Two scriptures come to mind, and make a divine connection together in my head. Those scriptures are "Faith is the substance of things hoped for and the evidence of things not seen" (Hebrews 11:1) and the other is "all things work together for the good of those who love God and are the called according to his purpose" (Romans 8:28). I believe that we are all called in some manner, and we just have to have faith that whatever we encountered will at some point serve as a catalyst to shift the atmosphere for the betterment of our being.

Day 47

DON'T GET IN THE RING

Many times we think that we are going to win every time we get into a battle with the enemy. We have to understand that he knows our weakness and will use that to play against us. Knowing this, please remember that if you think that you are going to win every time there is no need to get in the ring because there will be battles that you will fight and seem to have lost. That is the reality that is not preached often enough. Due to the fact that no one wants to tell you that reality, we are being set up for failure because we always see winning as the bad guy being down. The enemy is never down and he never quits. Have you ever thought of what the enemy does when he sees himself as losing the battle with you. He keeps throwing additional obstacles. The strategy behind that is to overwhelm you and get you so discombobulated that you can't focus on the fight because you are so used to dodging the bullets, so to speak. Winning does not mean that the enemy is down for the count, its means that you have matured to the point of counting the costs of the opposition and you become unbothered to his tactics and to stay focused on your praise.

I DIDN'T REALLY BELIEVE

He kept telling me…. but I didn't believe him….God told me he would see me through, but I didn't believe him. I shouted with the best of them but believed him partially based on the lying elements of my past. I said I had faith, but I wavered every time. I was scared to admit it because many would say I wasn't a Christian and would doubt my witness, but God. Today God, I share with you the intimacy of my heart that there are times when I am scared. There are times I read your words and I REALLY want to believe, but my humanity speaks louder than your still soft voice. I need the roar of your love to speak to my unbelief and remind me numerous times of your undying love for me. Though you show me continuously, please open my eyes that I may be more sensitive to your presence. I love you God and after all is said and done I just want to please you.

HE IS IN CONTROL

We often state that God is in control and we are often speaking of the situations and circumstances that we are in, but God is in control of more than that. He is in control of people and has a way of making people do what he wants them to do, even when they don't want to, He is in control to make people bless you when they don't want to, and even make us bless people we don't see as worthy of our blessing. Stop underestimating the power of God's influence in your live as well as the lives of others. God is not a God that can be boxed in, in any manner. You are limited, he is limitless. Take the limits off of him and watch him work.

ILLUMINATION OF EXPOSURE

The word of God will illuminate the good and the bad, the wise and the foolish, and is the best tool that we can use to learn the best possible way to live. We have to be careful of drawing too much light to others wrongs because our own darkness can be exposed as well. I love the fact that the ground around the cross was leveled meaning that all of us have sinned and falling short and no one sin is greater than another. I marvel at the fact that many are so quick to ostracize others for their sin, but fail to see the fatality of their own lack of restraint and their ability to stumble into darkness or sin. More word, less falling! Notice I said "less falling," not "no falling" because there is a reason that we have to die daily in our flesh because in it no good thing dwelleth. Equip and empower others with the word of God and teach them how to use the word of God which is the sword! Use the light of the Word to illuminate the love of God that supersedes all darkness that we will encounter.

Day 51

I MISSED IT!

They say you never miss you water til your well runs dry. Though this is an earthly cliché; it could definitely have a spiritual revelation to it. This is going to be a hard lesson so brace yourself. Many times we don't understand the causes and effects that we endure because we are so busy crying about the consequence. For every action there is a reaction, and for every cause there is an effect. Do you think that you got away with your action without dealing with its consequences? GOD FORBID! Yes, God forgives your act, but the lesson is your consequence. If you miss the consequence, you are almost sure to repeat the action so I urge you, don't miss it for heaven sake.

Day 52

You Don't Know What it Feels Like to be Me!

Years ago, I wrote a song entitled, "You Have No Clue." I was inspired to write this song because many people THOUGHT they knew me and they felt that they could handle me any kind of way because of that fact or shall I say assumption. Many people look at my accomplishments and think that they want to be me, but they fail to count the costs of the oil of this anointing on my life. God has graced me to make this life of mine look easy, but walk a day in my shoes and see the complexity that is me. There are things that I have been through and sacrifices that I have to make that have even made me second guess my own self purpose and destiny though I know that I know that I know what God has called me to do. I urge you today to stop looking at the lives of others and desiring to be them because clearly there are some hidden sacrifices that had to be made and so it is with you in your life. What sacrifices are you willing to make to be all that God has called you to be?

PROPHETIC, NOT PROPHONY

It is time out for the phony prophetic words given, because you know me. I am looking for the authenticity of your words followed by your actions. Many times we receive words from people who know us and know the desires of our heart and they speak to us in hopes of giving us motivation to do better and want better or in the words of Jesse Jackson, "to keep hope alive!" God is calling us to a place of maturity where we don't run with itching ears, but with the earnest hearts that run after God and not the gifts.

Day 54

I SURVIVED

I survived all of that for such a time as this. Many times we focus on the issues of life and sometimes we even have a tendency to rehearse the pain that we have been through but fail to appreciate the purpose. We should be prepared to remember that;

Pain+Purpose=Passion

But for others your passion feeds your purpose and in turn speaks directly to their pain. So the next time you go through your storm, remember it's not for you, but that someone else may be helped. Just remember you survived for a reason, to be a blessing!

Day 55

I'M FEARFUL IN SAFE PLACES

Many people have created acronyms for the word "fear." For this purpose I am creating

> F-forever
> E-entertaining
> A-Adverse
> R-Reactions

And this is a reality that we face no matter where we are, even in the safest places like in our bedrooms and secret closets. Today I challenge you to adopt a new acronym to state

> F-forever
> E-executing
> A-anointed
> R-revelations

Walk in the faith that is ordained by God, and move forward in a manner that pleases God. For without faith it is impossible to please God.

I'M THINKING MYSELF HAPPY

There are always times when we just have to think attacks and it forces us in our minds to think. Whatever you choose to think can determine your mindset. I personally try to think positively. When I do I find myself thinking myself happy. What do I think about? I'm glad you asked! I think about all the times I didn't think I could make it or take it, BUT GOD! I think about the times I didn't know how I would make it through, BUT GOD! The times I didn't see a way, nor was a way being made for me and I couldn't even make a way, BUT GOD! The times friends became foes and family abandoned me, BUT GOD! I dare you to think yourself happy and create your own happy place of peace, praise and blessings. Come on and think yourself happy.

Day 57

AGAIN, A GAIN

There are times that we have been taught that it is negative to have to repeat a thing. I remember one time I was on a conference call and we were having testimony service, so to speak, and one lady kept saying I went through this and I went through that and I said, "Lord not again!" she said. My spirit was punctured by the word "again" and it changed the very element of my being. In that time God spoke to me and said, "Please let her know that to do a thing again is not bad as long as there is a gain. As an educator, I transferred this revelation not only to my life, but also to my classroom. I remind my students it's not always a matter of if you got it all right or all wrong, but the gain in knowledge that you make each time. So remember, as long as you're again comes with a gain, rest assured God is pleased with your progress and you should be proud of yourself.

Day 58

REVELATION IS ESSENTIAL

A revelation is a revealed word from the Lord. Revelation is what makes one marvel at the fact that they have read and/or encountered a thing on more than one occasion and each time they get something new and/or different than they did the last time. It's just like watching a mystery for the first time and you have no clue the answer to the mystery, but then when you watch it the second time, you begin to see the little clues that makes it all make sense. So it is with revelation! You read a scripture and it seems pointless, but then you begin to live it out and you begin to see the scripture come to life in your living. Then the fun part is the more you live, the more you encounter, and the more your perspective of the lesson unfolds. So as you read your Bible, just think of it as a life tank and though you may not need it now, keep living and it will come in handy and as the old folks used to day, you will understand it better by and by.

WHAT'S THE ADDRESS?

I remember when I was in seminary, I was told that in reference to scripture; if you can't "cite" it, don't say it. What they were trying to convey is that if you cannot tell the location of the scripture, then don't mention it. Years after that encounter, God gave an even greater revelation, as well as the traditional play with words that he and I have and he said, "If you can't 'sight' it don't say it!" Revelation is that if people can't see you trying to live it out, and then don't speak it out. Does it mean that you will fully apprehend it? No! But what it does say is that, I am trying to live this thing out the best I can. Let people sight the scripture that you are citing.

A FISH ROTS FROM THE HEAD DOWN

Stinking living usually is the result of stinking thinking. If your mind is jacked up, so will your decisions and your relationships be. If there is damage to your emotions that you have not sought healing for, everything you do will be affected by your inability to think logically and coherently because of your damaged emotions. You've been hurt and you've been wounded, join the rest of the world, we all have been hurt and wounded but you don't stay there. Get back up, renew your mind and stop running in circles. You have purpose, but you may never know it as long as the damage to your emotions decays your thought life. Fix your stinking thinking and let's go!

JUST GET UP!!

There are days when God gives us a direction and the problem is that many of us just want to lay on it and wait for the inheritance. Many people say that my insomnia drives them crazy, but then God revealed to me that it's my insomnia that made me successful because just as the virtuous woman did, she was up while it was still night preparing to make provisions for her family. Most people who are authentically successful, they work more than they sleep and slumber and even when they are home and chilling, their brains are working towards the expected end of success. So what are you waiting for? What is the promise that God has for you to fulfill that you have been sitting on? Sit no longer, just get up and do it!

THE SQUEAKY STEP

When I would go to my grandmother's house she had some wooden steps. As we tried to walk, the squeaking step would get on my nerves and I always thought that it was this one particular step and then one day I realized that it was the step that I left. So it is in the spirit realm.... successful people should always be able to tell you that people talking about them is normal on their steps to their destiny because the people that you leave are often the ones who talk about you the worst because you are doing something that they would not dare to do. Don't lose focus due to the squeaking steps of your circle. Keep walking and pursuing your destiny. Guess what? The steps never stop squeaking. As long as you keep moving, you fix one step, and then another will squeak, but don't let the naysayers deter you. Keep walking.

Day 63

DON'T CONFUSE PROBLEM, PROCESS AND PURPOSE

There are three p's in life that we often misconstrue; problem, process, and purpose. In a manner of revelation all three are vital to Christian maturity and growth. Problems are the catalyst to the process that is needed for us to pursue our purpose with passion. If you leave out any of these elements the other loses its savor and impact. The way to stay focused during the trials and tribulations that you go through is to remember that in order to get through any problem, we must process it by finding its revelation which is the reason why we had to go through the thing in the first place and then tie it to your purpose and continue in the passion that is needed to serve effectively in the kingdom.

LIVING ON PURPOSE

As I mature in my life I have made a conscious decision to live my life on purpose. For so long, I done what everyone else thought that I should do and would find myself either accidentally happy or intentionally miserable. Right around 40 I decided to change that and I intentionally make sure that I am happy first. This made life better for me as well as the others around me. I found myself happier in my skin, but I also found myself emotionally available for a fulfilling relationship in every capacity. My decision to live on purpose helped me to take a stand and make a conscious decision as to my boundaries within relationships. What were my deal breakers and what it was that I was willing to compromise on was just some of the things that I learned during this time. Take the time today to make some decisions in your life and live your life on purpose with the intention to be happy.

Day 65

KNOWING AND STUDYING
THE STRATEGY OF THE ENEMY

Oftentimes, as believers, we are taught to learn the ways of God which is never a bad thing, but what it does is creates an obscure obstruction to successful warfare strategies which leads us to defeat when wrestling with the enemy. Many of us are taught to hold our peace and let the Lord fight our battles. Beware this is a cliché and totally against the revelation of the power of the tongue and mindset. We have to think clearly and speak intentionally, almost demandingly over the prosperity of our lives. In order to do that, you have to study to know the strategy and tactics of the enemy. This comes with time, experience and maturity. Strategically, it is our duty to ensure that we are not crying over the same spilled milk of yesterday. What trips us up today should soon be overcome and filed away in our experience bank. What doesn't kill you really does make you stronger in the faith.

TIME OUT, TOUCH DOWN

As children, time out has a negative connotation to it. As we mature especially in the faith, we learn that our spiritual walk includes critical points of time outs. We have to take that time out of our busy lives to have an encountering touch from God that speaks to the very element of our being and forces us to fall down on our faces and worship him like never before. Time out produces the opportunity for us to experience his touch and to bow down in worship which will serve as a catalyst to our spiritual growth and maturity in our faith and relationship with him.

THE SPEARHEAD OF DESTRUCTION

Herod, who was the spearhead to the failed attempt to destroy Jesus, tried for many years and literally died trying to do it. Listen people of God, whatever is for you, is for you, and no devil in hell can take it from you but what he can do is create a distraction that will ultimately act as the spearhead to your destruction. We have all seen or heard of the movie Fatal Attraction. For Kingdom sake, let's put a spin on that title and call our experiences of this type as Fatal Distractions. The thing that the devil knows is your weakness is what he will use to distract you. If you are single, he will use the "dream man or woman", if you are fasting, he will cause you to get meal invites, you get my drift. The point is that you have to be sober and vigilant for the adversary like a roaring lion, walketh about seeking whom he may devour, distract, deter, and bring to their demise. Watch out, because he wants to destroy you.

Day 68

THE CAMOUFLAGE OF CHAOS

Chaos is often the camouflage for the catalyst to your blessing. Will you drown in the chaos, or will u be compelled to move forward? Have you ever noticed that every time you are seeking the face of God intensely, chaos and commotion is sure to follow? It comes as another form of distraction. Chaos is created to drown out the still small voice that is the God and to keep you from getting direction and instruction from the father. You have to command the chaos to clear out and quiet your spirit so that your mind, body, spirit, and soul can connect and reproduce the directions that is given to you from the father.

Day 69

I SEE YOU AND I SEE YOU

When encountering things in life, you have to use your spiritual 20/20 vision. That is that you see things with your spiritual discernment as well as your natural eye. That means seeing what people say as well as what they don't say. To see what they are doing as well as get a spiritual revelation of the motive for their action. That's when you can say, "I see you and I see you!" The reason why discernment is critical is because it not only allows you to see not only the physical manifestation of it, but also the spiritual revelation of it as well. The effect of this knowledge is that it will educate you on how to deal with not only the individual but the spirit that they are operating in as well. This is Kingdom minded revelation.

HE'S GOING TO MAKE IT ALL WORTH IT

As a single woman, my one dream and desire is to meet my Mr. Forever and to be held in his arms and be able to exhale from the core of my being to say, "For this, it was all worth it!" So it is when we go through our storms. We may not understand all that is going on in the meantime, but when the storm is over, we should be able to look back at it and say, "It was all worth it!" The great thing about life is that we are ever learning, but once we know our purpose and calling, from that moment on, we should see the storms that we go through as a piece of the puzzle that will complete and amplify our calling and purpose. We must understand that everything that we go through is not for us anyway, it is for others. Seeing people delivered and set free from the transparency of our testimony is the great exhale that we sigh when we say, "He made it all worth it!"

IN THE MIDST OF MY MESS

God Thank You! Thank you for loving me in the midst of my mess! Thank you for blessing me in the midst of my mess! Thank you for using me in the midst of my mess! Thank you for choosing me in the midst of my mess! Thank you that my mess is creating my message. My tests are creating my testimony! When I feel less than, it actually proves to be a lesson in humility and even more so humanity. I admit, God, that there are times that I feel lost in my mess, but the most important appreciation that I have is that you never left me in the midst of my mess.

Day 72

I WON'T LOSE MY IDENTITY

In life we all operate in various roles starting out as children, and then we become siblings. Later we increase responsibilities to become parents. This same increase of responsibility and additional identities also apply to the level of accountability and growth in Christendom. You start off as a babe that sits and soaks up everything that is being said and done and you pretty much go with the flow because you don't know much difference yet. The criticality of this is that it is during that phase that many have a tendency to lose their identity. They begin listening to the religious rhetoric that says that you have to give up this and you have to do that but they never make any deposits to tell you what you can do and how to evolve into your new self. This is how the loss of identity takes place. There comes a time though when you must mature and ask God for your own spiritual identity; your gift, your purpose, your place in the body. Don't allow Christendom and the religious sect to make you lose your identity make that great exchange from your old man to your new man with Christ and him alone.

When Jesus Passed My Past and Talked to My Destiny

You say you know my past, but what you missed is when Jesus passed and not only healed me, but made me whole because I continued to praise and worship him despite my circumstances. Many people feel as though they know you based on their PAST experiences with you. They fail to realize that the past that they think they know is actually the tests of God to get you to a greater place of passion in him. Those mistakes that they smear in your face are the building blocks that were necessary for your spiritual growth and maturity. Let's take it a step further, not only your spiritual growth and maturity but your natural growth as well. Just as Christ passed by your past when he cast it into the sea of forgetfulness, but takes those lessons that you attained to develop you and usher you into your place of purpose and destiny that is also what you should look for in the cloud of witnesses that are around you.

Day 74

YOUR COMFORT WILL NOT CONFLICT
WITH MY DESTINY

Sometimes God's elevation of you and your life makes others uncomfortable. Their discomfort is what produces the behavior that we call "hating." Can we look at the revelation of this term? First of all "hating" comes from a place of jealousy and discomfort. They are jealous at the fact that you dare to be different, and discomfort in the fact that because you chose to take the path to excellence, it is the manifestation of the choice that they made to stand still. Don't allow others to make you feel some kind of way because they are uncomfortable. When people used to persecute me for my educational accomplishments, I would allow it to get to my spirit and I would find myself dumbing down my personality to not look as smart as God has blessed me to be. I remember one conversation with a Bishop and he spoke words that changed my outlook. He said to remind people that there are still seats in the school house for them. The seats are comfortable in class, but the outcome creates a comfort that can't be taken away and that is the knowledge that you acquire that will keep you from your current place of discomfort.

Day 75

THIS IS NOT ME!

At some point in life we have to realize when someone is taking us out of character. Not the character of you, but the character of Christ. You may not believe this, but many people will hear of your witness and will intentionally try you just to get you out of character so they can say foolish things such as, "Uh huh, see I knew you wasn't that saved!" as if they just caught you doing something ungodly. Now the disclaimer to this whole word for the day is that there is an accountability that we are held to, but on the same token, be mature enough to know that you are still in the form of flesh and yes, you are going to sin, and yes you will get angry. The key to the matter is knowing your limitations and removing yourself from situations and people that can and will take you out of your element of peace. We have to know our limitations and the things that try us and provoke our fleshly reactions. I always say that I know I am getting better and growing because it wasn't long ago that I would lash out and give you all that business in 2.2 seconds and now that I am up to the ability to count to ten, which takes longer than the normal 2.2 seconds, it also gives me the ability to walk away or come up with a more productive answer that may not even involve curse words. Look at the growth of God!

I Made it Without...

Without a mom, without a dad without a cheerleader, sometimes without any earthly inspiration, but I made it through the grace of God. People ask me all the time what drove me to the degrees, the books, the cds, the career and all of the many other things that I do, especially when no one in my family, on either side, has accomplished any of these things. My response is always this, "I cannot help the drive and desires of my kindred, but I always knew I was one of my kind." My mother was one of 6 girls and they all chose their own roads in life. Five of the six of them had children, and we all have chosen our own roads in life but most of them are all career driven and many are entrepreneurs. We, as cousins, did all of that without...! We had no role models for the businesses that we are in, we are all believers in Christ and we all have our own story to tell. We have one aunt left and I just believe that that she was left here with us to enjoy seeing the lineages continue and blossom. I know there are times that I look at our family tree and marvel at the greatness of God and the favor that he has over our lives and in our family. The most powerful thing is that we made it without....!

SIZE DOES MATTER

I can't be big when little has got me! Your achievements are only as large or small as your perception to achieve them. If your vision is small so shall your productivity be. What can pull you out of that mode? Vision, perseverance, encouragement and desire to do above and beyond what you can ask or think as well as what you are used to. Your vision should always supersede what you see in your surroundings. As I have walked through life, I have always sought to see where I can make a difference in whatever situation that I am in. I always seek to see where I can lend a hand to make an impact. Not ever really seeking self-glory or fame, but just to be a blessing and in that spirit is where my influence has come. Have you ever reflected on your life as a kid and the dreams you had back then and how those dreams have come to past or not? I have always been a lover of learning and so in that I always knew I wanted to be a teacher. However, I never knew that you could be a doctor of education. I always only knew doctors to be in medicine. I remember as a kid I would always see my mother writing on this book about her life, who would have thought that I would be the only published author in our family. All I am trying to say is that when you speak of the word that says, "exceedingly and abundantly above all that you can ask or think." It's great to see it, good to read it, but greater to live it.

WHEN IN PURSUIT FOR THE POWER, BE PREPARED FOR THE PAIN

Oftentimes, we ask God to enlarge our territory, and we fail to prepare for the pain that is associated with it. We ask for patience and we get trials. We ask for anointing, we get purification through the purifying fire. We ask for relationships, we get the hurdles and obstacles that we must overcome to attain that. All in all, whenever we ask for increase of any sort, we have to be prepared for the pain, discomfort and/or obstacles that we have to overcome to attain that increase. When we see the people of influence and power, it is our first instinct to say, "I can do that" when the truth of the matter is that the statement should end with a question mark instead of an exclamation point. The reason for the question is because it remains to be seen whether or not you can take the issues that it took to get them to that point. Can you take the lying, the backbiting, the ridicule, the persecution? Remember that for every level that you rise to in life, there are obstacles that you have to overcome first. So before you ask for increase, please remember to count the cost!

WHEN BAD LOOKS GOOD

There are times when we go through barren places that make bad look good. When I say that, I am speaking of all levels of life. One familiar to many is when we choose romantic relationships that, if we were not barren and lonely, we would never choose them for ourselves. We settle for things that we would normally run from. We allow behaviors that we feel are deplorable. We fight for the relationship/companionship and lose sight of the peace that God provides, especially to the single. I am not bashing anyone, but the reality is that when we want a thing bad enough we will do anything to attain, to maintain, and to retain it. This is when bad looks good. If you ever find yourself in this place, I dare you to seek the face of God and his desires for your life and focus on this, "If it jeopardizes your peace, the price is too high!"

WHERE AM I?

If you just take a moment, no matter what you're going through, and just begin to think of where you could be versus where you are, I promise you that you will find your place of peace and gratitude realizing that it could be worse than it looks. Every year I set personal goals, ministry goals and financial goals. These goals all coincide with my life goals for myself. When I take the time to review the status of my life goals, I ask the question, "Where am I?" This comes when you live life intentionally and on and in purpose. All things that I do in my life should tie right in to my life purpose and destiny. When is the last time that you took the advice of scripture and wrote your vision and made it plain that others may see it and run with you or run away from you? Reevaluate where you are in relation to where you want to be and stay on track allowing nothing to deter you.

THANK YOU

There are times in our life when we owe a huge thank you to the ones who hated us, the ones who talked about us, the ones who refused to believe in us. It was a great scripture that said it was good that I was afflicted. The revelation of this is that had it not been for that malice, doubt, hate, jealousy or contention, you may not be as motivated as you are to reach your goals and aspirations. Finding and fulfilling your purpose may not be a priority had it not been for the opposition that came to you in the form of life. Life! I honor you! Life! I praise God for every crossroad and obstacle that you brought my way. Life! You took so much from me only to give it back to me in a greater form. Thank You!

MAJOR/MINOR

We often hear the saying, "making a mountain out of a molehill" which in turn tells us not to major in the minor things and minor in the major. However, it takes discernment to know the difference. In my relationship book, I talk about the things that are considered deal breakers and communicators. Deal breakers are the things that threaten your sense of peace and security; however communicators are the things that can be overcome with a strong foundational premise of communication. Many obstacles that we face in life can be overcome by simply communicating with the involved parties and those are the minor things. The major things are the matters that can leave a hole in your heart and mind and close your perception of others after encountering them. A relationship that is filled with lies, deceit, secrets and infidelity are major because even with communication, in my eyes, these things cannot be overcome not only because it assassinates the trust in the relationship, but also because it has a lasting effect even on future relationships to come. That is when you know it is major, when it effects more than just the parties involved. Minor issue are things such the division of labor in the household, the bad habits that we have such as leaving the caps off of the toothpaste or leaving the toilet seat up. It has no bearing on anyone but the immediate parties involved and honestly these are matters that you look back on and laugh. So know the difference and act accordingly.

PURPOSE, NOT PROBLEMS

The things that I go through are not really problems when I understand that they are all working toward my purpose. Changing your perspective on the issues of life is all about maturity and growth. This is when a word becomes rhema and revealed in a real way. It is no longer just words on a page, but a reality of life. It's the blessed assurance that we often sing about that says no matter what I go through, I know I serve the same God that brought me out of the last issue to bring me through this one as well. Remember that everything that you go through is all about purpose and preparation for the next level of glory that you are about to experience. So don't curse it, embrace it and know that it all works for your good.

THE BUCKET WITH THE HOLE IN IT

You cannot fill a bucket with a hole in it! If you are locked in the ways and days of your past, I can only pray for you and keep it moving because someone out there is dying to be delivered for real. What I had to learn in the early days of my ministry, but that I honestly still struggle with due to the fact that I am loyal to a fault, is to let people reside where they desire. We oftentimes, want more for others than they want for themselves and so therefore we fight harder for them than they fight for themselves. We have to be careful to convey the potential that we see in them to them and then stand back and watch them fight for it and when we see their effort then it is our duty to assist. The error comes in when we see their potential and then fight for it to come to past while they watch and complain and often times fight against us. Be a bucket filler by sowing into the lives of others, but make sure that the bucket doesn't have a hole in it.

Day 85

You Didn't Start It...

He began a good work in me that has nothing to do with you. There are times when God will orchestrate the severance of relationships and the shutting of doors in your life to ensure that no one gets the glory but him. Many times as we elevate in life many people want to take the credit for it and they put things and people in your life that can be used as a catalyst to the things that God has in store for you. The issue comes in when they think that you can't reach the level of greatness that you are destined to reach through the grace of God without them. WRONG! These are the moments when you have to share that HE who has begun a good work in ME is FAITHFUL to perform his will in my life with or without your assistance. The thing that they fail to realize is that God will force them to bless us, even when they don't want to. That alone should serve as a reminder to them that says, "You didn't start it, but he will finish it!"

Day 86

I'm Scared

Humanity produces an emotion called fear. Fear is a very healthy and normal emotion and can be a positive indicator to the authenticity of your humanity. There are things that scare you in its beginning stages, but if you just hold on and see the salvation of the Lord and I promise you that it will work out. Then there is the fear and trembling that happens when you show reverence for God. For instance, I was called to preach at the age of 7 and have been preaching since I was 9 and every single time that I am up to preach or sing or do anything for God, I get scared. For others, it may be entering into your first relationship after a bad experience; there is a fear and anxiety that comes about with that as well. As a teacher, I know that I am a committed educator that gives my all, but every time on test day for my students, I get scared. All I am trying to say is that fear is normal and healthy and manifests in many forms but the greatest thing is that fear also provokes a complete reliance on God!

DON'T TOUCH ME

Joseph never touched Mary while she was pregnant with the promise. He was ever so careful not to penetrate the purpose that was Jesus, even if he didn't understand it. We should look for the same characteristics in our earthly mate. Start the relationship off with communication and expectation that says, "I'm still under construction. I'm still a work in progress." Don't touch me is not only physically, but also mentally, emotionally and the like. It means don't do anything to penetrate nor interfere with my purpose in Him. Don't put your mouth on what I know to be God's purpose for my life. Yes, there must be balance and there must be awareness of the needs of your mate but don't lose your identity nor deter your purpose to please them and disappoint God. Please God first and all other things will be taken care of.

GLEAN BEHIND THE REAPERS

Don't get in front of them, but sit back and watch what the Lord is saying to do. Reapers will show you how to get to where you want to be with the least amount of obstacles. I was one of those children that I didn't have to do what everyone else did to see the results and consequences of their actions. I was one to let them go ahead of me and make all the mistakes and I see what it did to them and so from THEIR experience I knew what to and not to do. I saw what worked and did not work for them and I made up in my mind the route that I would take. From that mindset and way of life, I literally learned how I wanted to be as well as how I didn't want to be. Watching their achievement and drive gave me the tenacity to say, "I will not stand behind a parked car in the spirit." I want to be amongst those that have vision and dreams and aspirations. Those who are headed somewhere and don't mind sharing the transparency of their being with me whether they knew it or not I called it "gleaning behind the reapers." The ones who plant good seed into fertile ground and are sure to get a result, that's my type of crowd.

WHEN GOD SAYS NO

We all know what to do when God says "Yes", but we have a tendency to struggle when he says "No." He tells us that his grace is sufficient for whatever we go through, but we often times have trouble accepting his no's and not now's. This is because we don't allow room for his perfect will and provision for our lives. If the truth be told many of us seek a reward for the few minutes that we live right. It's a sense of spiritual entitlement. In so many words and ways we say, "Lord I have been good this season, don't you think I deserve....?" Can I tell you that this mindset is a form of spiritual prostitution and manipulation and we all know that the God we serve cannot and will not be manipulated in that manner. It is almost like our earthly children, when they do something good or say something nice to us, the first thing we do is ask them what it is they want and we watch how their reaction change when we say no. So it is with Christ. With this analogy in mind and the maturity that comes with life and experiences, I am getting better at accepting his "No" realizing it's probably his way of protecting me.

Day 90

I'm Not Through Living it Yet!

Many people tell me that I should write a book about this and a book about that especially when it comes to my life, but my response is, "I'm not through living it yet." Not that I can write it after I'm dead but what it means is that I cannot write about a season until that season is complete and not only complete, but I must get a revelation of the season. See there is a danger in writing the final chapter when you are still living it. It's almost like writing about giving birth and you are still pregnant with your first child. You cannot truly articulate the pain, because you haven't experienced it. You cannot tell about the length of the labor, because it hasn't occurred. I urge you today to please don't try to testify about a test that you are still taking, it will prove to be ineffective and not authentic but more so, it will be incomplete and helping no one.

Spiritual Versus Sensual

Many times we find ourselves trying to reason with a person who is operating in their senses when clearly we, as believers, operate in the spiritual. This is especially true in the single life and dating world. One of my greatest struggles is trying to explain my need for spiritual companionship to a person who only sees me for the hips and dips of my body. This is also true in all other elements of life as well. We as believers see the benefit and beauty on obstacles while others see them as inconveniences and punishments of life. To explain our spiritual revelations to a carnal mind is not only impossible, but meaningless because they will never understand it. So stay in your lane and live in your truth and don't veer off from your predestined path that God has you on. Stay spiritual and win others over by the testimony that you have.

Day 92

HOW LONG 'TIL WE BECOME ONE?

Do you know how many people are married and are yet to become one? How many people are in relationships and are not one? How many people who work together in ministry and are not one? To be one has nothing to do with agreeing with one another on frivolous matters, but the matters that really matter such as spiritual things, such as vision and aspirations, goals and dreams. Things that matter on a spiritual level, things that matter in heaven and that terrify devils here on earth. Scripture says, "Can two walk together except they agree?" I feel that heaven and earth says, "NO!" The reason being is because where there is no agreement, there is no harmony. Where there is no harmony, then harm is produced, be it to the lives and the well-being of each other or the ones that are around them. Becoming one is so much more than just agreement, it is about productivity. Take your time and become one with yourself and then become one with another therefore all elements will be aligned both in heaven and in earth.

BECAUSE I KNOW WHO I AM!

Many people ask how I walk around like an average person when my name is in lights and I have many attributes and achievements to my name. My answer is always the same and that is "because I know who I am." When I say that, it is in all humility because I mean that I know who I am in Christ. See in my flesh no good thing dwelleth and so knowing who I am in my flesh is what is dangerous and is fed by external matters of this world. I am saying that I know who I am in Christ which is no one in myself, but everything in him. It is in him that I live, move and have my being. Everything that I am is in him and everything that I can do is because of him. This assurance keeps me humble because I know that outside of him, all of my endeavors would fail from the businesses to the education to the careers and shonuf the ministry would be for naught. Knowing who you are means so much more when you keep it in perspective. Know who you are internally and let the external factors go because one feeds the flesh and produces pride, while the other feeds the spirit and produces maturity.

POSITION YOURSELF

One of the most amazing things about life is when a baby comes into existence. The cycle in which it grows and begins to form and develop is amazing. However, I think that the way in which they enter into the world is painfully breathtaking. Do you realize that a baby has no sense of time or concern when they are within the womb? They are the purest form of the modern day Adam and Eve. They are naked and they don't know it. They have no sense of need, lack or time. All of its needs are met without them really asking. They have cravings that are all their own and even those are often met without them saying a word. But the interesting thing is that they know how to get in position when they are preparing to be born. Yes I understand scientifically the body has something to with it and I also understand that there are some exceptions, but for the most part it is an innate process that happens naturally. My question is why is it that we who are outside of the womb have such issue with positioning ourselves to be used of the Lord which is an innate motivation but babies can. Babies get into position innately how about you?

Day 95

THE PROPHETIC REVELATION OF CHRISTMAS

There are many elements of Christmas that are traditional, but when I sought the Lord he gave me a revelation for many of the elements and what they mean to the life of the believer;

- The tinsel/garland represents the lessons I refused to learn so as the children of Israel did I had to go around and around the mountain until the lesson was attained.
- The star/salvation equates to the shifting of the atmosphere as it was the star that served as the catalyst to the wise men that Jesus was born and led them to the decision to assist in the saving of the life of Jesus.
- The tree represents the tree planted by the water, it shall not be moved.
- The ornaments/bulbs are the obstacles we had to face that popped up periodically in our lives, but when you look from the outside in, it looks beautiful, but from the inside out, it can become cumbersome.
- The gifts are the seasonal support that you get from others in your life. More love is shown during the holiday season than any other time of year and the gifts often times don't make it to the next year, which is the same as some relationships.

- The lights are representative of some of the Christians that we are and the actions that we exhibit;
  - o Flicker-on again/off again- The inconsistent relationship that the immature Christian has with Christ.
  - o Chasing- The way we should be with him, ever chasing after him (Jesus).
  - o Singing-The people who are crippled by the absence of music, but come to life and to church only for the music

Pick your holiday décor wisely and let it be a reflection of your relationship with him.

EXHAUSTED EMOTIONS

Don't be moved by exhausted emotions. When you get tired, you can't trust how you feel! Your emotions will send you false signals. Your perceptions will be on overload and will throw you off kilter. This is why we must rest in him and ensure that he has spoken to us in our secret place with him. This counteracts the exhaustion of the emotions that we are using to make decisions. Never make decisions when you are exhausted and never let your emotions rule your everyday actions. Exhaustion is the fuel and emotions are the flame and put together at the wrong time and in the wrong environment they can be combustible and harmful.

Day 97

THE SIGHT OF THE SUCCESSOR

When reading the story of Elisha and Elijah in the Bible (2Kings 2:9-15), we are taught what I call the 5 Ps of power. These 5 Ps have to be present in order for your leadership to be effective. First of all the Prophecy has to come forth from the Lord. Secondly, one has to persevere through the storms and obstacles that come to deter one from their destiny. Thirdly, the persecution has to come to make fool proof of your leadership abilities which leads us right in to the fourth point, passion. When the Passion is exhibited before the people the passing of judgement of others is less influential on your leadership skills and abilities. So be as Elisha and see the works of your predecessor and have sight of their dealings to see all of the things that you do and want to do when your turn comes.

<u>The 5 Ps of Power</u>

Prophecy
Perseverance
Persecution
Passion
Passing

THIS IS NOT WHAT I THOUGHT
"THERE" WOULD FEEL LIKE

Have you ever prayed and believed God for a thing and you just knew that when you arrived "there" or got that all of your prayers will be answered? Have you found yourself saying, "God when this happens for me, I will be free! I will be whole! I will be set! I will have arrived "there" at that place I always dreamed. Then you get "there" and realize it's not all it's cracked up to be. Devastating right? Embarrassing? Disappointing? I am sure there are a bunch of other adjectives that one can think of to describe their "there" experience. The reason why this takes place is because "there" is not what you thought it would be. "There was a secret fantasy island that only existed in your mind. Come from over "there" and live "here" in this place and appreciate your current place in God.

THE ENEMY OF THE INNER ME

Sometimes our greatest enemy is we ourselves, and that is what I call the "inner me." The inner me is the one who always operates in what the eye can see, when the heart wants to operate in faith. When the eyes want to see God in a matter, the inner me always sees the opposition and the storm. When you as a person wants to mature, but the inner me wants to remain selfish and childish seeking things that are self-gratifying and contrary to the will and the way of God. Hush the mouth of the enemy that is made manifest through the doubting "inner me" and keep moving toward the destiny which God has promised you.

CLUTTER DIMINISHES CLARITY

Clutter in our lives diminishes the clarity of our spirit. I have this quirky fact about me. I cannot go into my home office and work until my entire house is straight and neat. Then and only then can I go in my office and work. I never understood this methodology about myself until I received this revelation. My clarity comes when, first of all, I know that my physical house is in order and then I can begin operating from my spiritual house and bringing you the revelation that you are enjoying in not only this book and the books of the past, but also in the books to come. Clearing out the clutter of your mind is also important if you are going to be productive for the kingdom. Clean out the clutter so that you can get the clarity that you need to be as effective as you can in whatever the endeavors are that you are doing.

IF YOU SAW MY FIRE,
YOU WOULD FEEL MY PRAISE

I remember in my earlier days in Christ, as a praise and worship leader, I would find myself frustrated because in the passion of praise and worship, I would see people just sitting there as if God owed them something. They would stand only because we said stand, they would clap upon demand, and they would move at the leader's request. I would find myself spiritually frustrated because I couldn't understand how they enjoyed and complimented me as their praise and worship leader and would often leave that portion of the service in awe of how God moved during our time together. They would often say things like, "You never miss a beat nor have a bad day where God don't move!" I would always stress to them that it was because my praise and worship don't begin at service, but it's a lifestyle that has brought me through various trials and tribulations of my life. The fire that you see now for God is a product of the fire that he brought me through in my life to produce the praise that you so easily enjoy.

MORE OF THIS MEANS MORE OF THAT

Many of us want increase but fail to count the costs of the increase. For a long time, many of us walked around quoting the prayer of Jabez that says, "Enlarge my territory..." but when the opposition arose we began to bind Satan and call all trials of the Devil. Well the truth of the matter is that not all trials are of the devil. Remember, he has to get the permission of the father to touch or even try you. So as we seek for more of anything, remember that more of what you want also means getting more of what you don't want. More money, more work! More patience, more trials! More love, more heartache to love someone through. Remember more of this means more of that!

TRANSITIONS

There is always room for change. Life is all about transitions as we go from glory to glory in God, but also as we go from one level to another on earth. Life is not a place for comfort zones because in the blink of an eye, things can and will change. Oftentimes, there are even times in which one catalyst for change can cause a ripple effect. For instance one bad decision of adultery can lead to divorce which will lead to a single household family and maybe leaving one person as a single parent which means increased work load and responsibility. Some changes and transitions in life we can control, and then there are others we have no control over, especially when it comes to matters of the Kingdom. Many times I have wanted to denounce my calling to ministry because I was tired and life's earthly transitions had worn me down. As much as I was ready to throw in the towel, God didn't make that transition an option. The best way to handle transition is to embrace it and understand that in order to grow in any manner, transition is inevitable.

Day 104

I CAN'T KEEP YOU COMPANY, THERE IS TOO MUCH FOR ME TO DO

There are many people in life who look at you and say that you are doing too much. They call you an overachiever or even have the audacity to tell you that, "It don't take all of that." The truth of the matter is they are probably right. It doesn't take all of that for them to sit on the stoop of do nothing and make nothing happen. Whatever you do, don't let the words of these kinds of people infiltrate your purpose, calling, or destiny. There is an old saying that says, "Misery loves company." Well here is a new one that is fresh off the press, "I won't board the plane of bored and do nothing, nor will I live on the street called stagnation." Listen, you have things to do. There are souls depending on you, so the next time you encounter this type of person just let them know I can't keep you company, I have too much for me to do.

Day 105

WHY? BECAUSE THERE IS NO AGREEMENT!

Many times people wonder why they seem to be in a wealthy place but there is no spiritual increase. Well, my friends, the reason why is because there is no agreement on the inside of your being. "I wish that you would prosper and be in health even as your soul prospers." When you prosper you should see that prosperity manifested in every area of your being. I remember when I was in full time ministry one of my spiritual advisers told me to sit still, be quiet and command that all of the elements of my being align with each other so that the word of the Lord can be revealed and manifested to my entire being. All the elements of your being are your mind, body, soul, spirit and intellect. I am sure we have all experienced the times when our spirit was instructed to do a thing, but our intellect had talked us out of it because we tried to understand a spiritual matter with an earthly mind. This is merely impossible which is why you have to be able to quiet all of your members and command them to all come under the subjection of the Holy Ghost so that they can all get the same instruction from God and act accordingly and on one accord.

Day 106

YOU CAN'T CROWN ME BEFORE YOU CROSS ME

Isn't it interesting that even Christ could not receive his crown before he was crossed by the very elect that he had in his circle. If we understand this truth then why is it that we get so out of character when we are betrayed and crossed by those that are closest to us? Sometimes the people that we are closest to are led to betray us because often times we have placed too much faith and trust in them and the only way through that is by experiencing the utmost betrayal. When betrayal comes it is often a servant of a lesson that we have placed too much faith in an earthly person and have lost our focus in Christ. We, as believers, are always screaming of how we are Christians which means to be Christ like, yet when we experience the things that Christ did we become discouraged and dismayed and often ready to throw in the towel. Remember if Christ couldn't be crowned before he was crossed, what more are we?

FROM RESIDUE TO RENEW

When we go through things, we are subject to have residue on us from that experience. It can manifest in the forms of unforgiveness, bitterness, and resentment just to name a few. There comes a time when you have to make a great exchange that releases the residue and allows one to be renewed by that experience. The Bible says to be not conformed to this world but to be ye transformed by the renewing of your minds. The renewing comes when you mature in a manner that allows us to see God in that experience. No, maybe that person was not your ideal mate, no matter how hard you tried to make that a fact or reality, but aren't you glad that you found out before it was too late. If you were just dating, aren't you glad you found out before you married them. If you were in a church that you knew was not of God because the manipulation was too strong, but aren't you glad that you accepted that truth before catastrophe struck and people were hurt or even killed. Maybe it's a job that you lost, that you felt you had to have the amount of money that they offered in order to survive. Aren't you glad that you got out and found something else before the scandals of that workplace was exposed? This is how you shift from residue to renew. Change your mind about the matter.

WHAT COMES AFTER MATURITY?

Many people feel as though they have arrived after they have matured
to a certain level. Especially in the natural realm, we always feel like things
are going to get better when we become, 13 (I'm a teenager), 15 (I can
drive), 16, (I can get a job), 18 (I am a legal adult), 21 (I can drink) and on
and on. The truth of the matter is that yes you have matured to that age or
milestone in your mind, but there is something that comes after maturity
and that is wisdom. Let wisdom have her perfect work. Maturity is defined
by reaching full development: perfected condition. Wisdom, on the other
hand, is defined as the quality or state of being wise; knowledge of what is
true and right coupled with judgment as to action; discernment, or insight.
In laymen's terms this means that maturity equates with the ability to do a
thing, but when wisdom talks about not only the ability to be able to do a
thing, but how to do a thing and when the right time and approach is. Let
wisdom be your guiding light. Maturity is nothing without the coupling
of wisdom. Let wisdom have her perfect work in your life and apply it in
every season of your life.

IT'S NOT JUST FOR ME!

Did you ever think that he called you in your mess to produce the message of life to proclaim his mandate on the life of someone else as well? What does this mean? It means that everything that you go through is not just for you, but for someone else as well. Just as Jesus needed the forerunning of John to do his work, you have to think, who are you the forerunner to? Who were you called to assist? Who are you going through what you're going through for? You do know it's not all about you, right? Nothing that we go through is just about us, but is for the sake of the kingdom. Just as nothing that Christ went through was for him but so that we can use him as an example in our lives. Seeing how he handled adversity, tribulation and humanity when it played against him, we can use him for an example for our own dealings. When you go through you various trials count it joy knowing that it's not just for you, but about others as well.

Day 110

I'M ANCHORED IN CHRIST NOT COMPANY

Sometimes isolation has to take place for the manifestation of Christ to be made. When we are surrounded by a crowd, it is easy to miss God because we can't hear him due to the chaos of the crowd. Many times we can be deceived by the voice of the people, or even our own voices and misconstrue it for the voice of God. This is why it is important for us to be anchored in Christ and not company. As we mature in Christ, we began to see things differently based upon our own revelation. Our circle of friends may become smaller as well. Sometimes it's because we are no longer led to follow the tradition as they may know it or that we may have experienced it in days prior. This reminds me of the time when I decided to go to a nondenominational seminary school which completely broadened my horizons on the matters of religiosity and spirituality. I lost a lot of friends because nowhere in the Bible did I see that we could not wear makeup, nor that we could not wear pants, and many other traditional methodologies that we were taught over time that turned out to be just that tradition. The truth of the matter is that I had to learn how to be ok being alone and without a cloud of friends and soon I came to enjoy it. Why? Because I am anchored in Christ and not Company.

Day 111

REMEMBER THERE ARE STEPS TO
YOUR PURPOSE AND DESTINY

As much as we may want to fly from one place in God to another, it's just not possible. We have to take the steps that are necessary for us to be successful in our walk with him. Those steps are ordered by him and our steps in our process may be very different than the steps of another. There are issues that one may need to deal with prior to their elevation that another does not. The reason for that is because we all have a different ministry to cater to and the needs of our demographic may be different from the other person's. For instance, two individuals may be called to the gift of evangelism. That gift does the same thing which is to win souls to Christ and bring them back to the local church body, but the way in which they are called to do it may be different. If one is talking to the unsaved market, they have never been to church or maybe don't even believe in God, the conversation and relationship may be completely different than the conversation that takes place between a backslider and an evangelist. This is why you have to embrace the steps to your destiny, because you never know where your path may lead.

I DIDN'T GET WHAT I WANTED

How many times have we become irritated when we didn't get what we wanted? We murmur and complain when things don't work out the way that we think they should. I know for the longest time I would cry, kick and scream like a spoiled kid when I didn't get what I wanted. However, when maturity hit me, I was able to appreciate the fact that what I wanted wasn't good for me. Though I sometimes don't get what I want, I always get what I need. The lesson in that is that I learned to thank God for his protecting me from myself and not honoring every request that I laid before him. It truly worked out for my good.

Day 113

YOU WILL WIN, IF YOU DON'T QUIT!

Don't quit no matter what! Don't know what to do? I tell you what not to do! Don't Quit!

Sick and tired of being sick and tired? Don't Quite! Broke, busted and disgusted? Don't Quit! Tired of the aching loneliness of being single? Don't Quit! Irritated with your job, your life, your marriage, and your children? Whatever you Do, Do NOT Quit! Though it seems hard to see at times, there is a blessing in the pressing of moving forward. All God wants is for you to keep moving and trust him. The game is already fixed, you have been declared the winner in the heavens so just know that you will win but you just can't quit!

CAN I JUST BE HONEST?

Oftentimes, we as believers live the lies that we are not supposed to tell. We fail to let the humanity in which we live shine through our religious façade. Let me pose a question to you. Have you ever thought of the fact that letting your humanity show may be all of the witness that potential converts needs to see? Think about it! What turns us off about most people is their inability to be real and honest. Well, what are you doing? Are you being unreal and dishonest? Shouting on the outside, hurting on the inside! Dancing in the church house and dodging the attacks that you profess to face in your own house. Just be honest!

If you hurt…hurt
If you're happy…be happy
If you're in pain….be in pain

Just be present and perfect in the fullness of your truth!

CAN YOU HEAR ME SCREAMING?
DON'T YOU KNOW I'M TIRED?

I'm tired y'all! Tired of being hurt! Tired of being broken! Tired of being deceived! Tired of wondering when the tired is going to end! I scream internally, hoping it can be heard externally! Tired of being alone! Tired of being dismayed! Tired of being discouraged! Tired of being strong when I want to be weak! Tired of acting happy when inside I'm broken into pieces! Listen, we all get tired but thank God for bearing our weariness and giving us the great exchange of strength for our HONEST emotion. Cast all your cares upon him!

I TRUST GOD EVEN WHEN HE SAYS NO!

Faith is developed in the midst of adversity when you have no choice but to believe God when your prayers are clearly not answered. It's a tough job that we all have to do. Trust him through the agony of his decline to meet what we believe to be our most dire need, let's be honest though. How many needs have we considered to be urgent? How many requests have we thought that we must have only to find that we were better off without them? How many senseless temper tantrums have we had only to come to the realization that our father really does know best. I said all of that to encourage you to continue to trust him even when he says, "No!"

IN THE MIDST OF MY "LIKE TO DIED" MOMENT!

How many times have we found ourselves quoting the chaotic cliché that says, "I like to died…" I like to died when I realized I lost my job! I like to died when I found out I was pregnant!

I like to died when my spouse left me for someone else. The truth of the matter is we didn't die, we lived, we survived, we overcame, and most importantly we were made the better because of it. I, myself, have used this saying a number of times, but as I have grown and matured, I realized that I say it less and less because I have really gotten the revelation that those, "like to died" moments really worked out for my good, and I choose to be better and not bitter, stronger, not sorrowful, sweeter and not more sour for the lemons that life has dealt me.

Day 118

SELF CAN'T HELP SELF ALL THE TIME

When will we get the revelation that in our flesh (self) no good thing dwelleth? When will it be understand that given the right situation and circumstances, even the upright will stumble and fall? No matter how hard we fast and pray and lay before the Lord the truth of the matter is that we still reside in our flesh. There is a reason why the scripture says that we must die to our flesh daily! Why? Because even God knows that we are likely to foul up the simplest task that he has given us to do. Why do you think he starts each new day with new grace and new mercy, because if there was a limit, we would all be lost? We have all said, "I couldn't help myself!" about one matter or another and this is the revelation of that famous saying, "Don't rely on self, rely on Christ."

I HAVE TO TRUST GOD WHEN I CAN'T TRACE GOD!

Have you ever received a promise from God and believed it with your whole heart that it was coming to pass only for the "deadline" in your mind to appear and there is still no manifestation? This, my dear friends is the point where you literally have to trust God and know that he is not slack concerning his promise. See many people are quick to tell you how he will give you the desires of your heart, but they forget the prerequisite that says to delight yourselves in him and acknowledge him in all your ways. So before you count him out and feel as though he's not meeting your needs trace him at the point of providence and know he is waiting for your part of the deal.

I DON'T KNOW!

We all quote scriptures about faith without getting the full reality or revelation of the matter which means that you have to walk in a place called, "I Don't Know!" In this very real land of uncertainty is where you will spend the majority of your lifetime. The land of "I Don't Know" exists based on the promises that his ways are higher than our ways and his thoughts are higher than our thoughts. Due to this reality, all we will ever really know is that he knows the plans that he has for us and we have to walk in that assurance. He said he will make our names great, but how? I don't know! He said he will give us the desires of our heart, but how? I don't know! I think you get my drift by now. Whatever your promise is from him, just accept it and move to the land of "I Don't Know!"

THINK GENERATIONALLY

Have you ever wondered why you do some of the things that you do? I, for one, am a stickler for organization and communication and I have always been that way. Well as I studied my family lineage, I realized the fact that my mother was one of six girls and each of the girls had their own responsibility. One was the cook, the other was the cleaner, and the other was the beautician and so on and so forth. Well my mother was the one that was responsible for the cleaning of the house. She brought us (my brother and I) up with the same responsibility and ensuring that our surroundings were to her standards of cleanliness and organization. Organized and cleanliness to me equates structure and in order to have structure, one must communicate. I raised my children in this same manner and belief and I see my daughter doing the same thing with my grandson. The point is don't just generalize everything as generational curses, but also think generationally as to why do you do the things you do both good, bad and indifferent.

Day 122

"BUSY"NESS IS THE KILLER OF PRODUCTIVITY

"I am busy!" you say. Ok, great but are you productive? Better yet are you divinely aligned in your pursuit to be busy? Is God breathing on your efforts to make you go from busy doing to being productive? Many of us feel as though the words busy and productive are interchangeable and the reality of it is that they are two completely different concepts. A person can be busy doing the wrong thing or doing the right thing at the wrong time, with the wrong people, for the wrong motive. All of these can be done and make you "look" busy. On the other hand, being productive means being God led to do a thing for the right reason, with the right motive, and intent with and for the right people. Check your schedule and make sure that you are productive and not just busy!

OBEDIENCE OPENS UP THE HEAVENS

How many times has God given us a thing to do at an appointed place and an appointed time? And for whatever reason we didn't do it. I am reminded of a time that God had instructed to go to my superior that morning when I arrived to work. I told God, "Why, I don't have anything to say?" Needless to say I didn't do it at that time, but I did it on my lunch break. Now for this particular instance, timing wasn't crucial, but the obedience was. When I finally went to her she told me that the school may be closing one of its campuses which means that staffing may very well be downsized. This is a great example of how God won't leave us blind to matters that concern us. So it wasn't about me needing to say something to her, but what she needed to say to me. How many times has the Holy Ghost unctioned you another way, be it a travel route, a financial decision, or a relationship matter? When you're obedient, he will withhold no good thing from you.

SHOUTING WITH CLOSED WINDOWS

He will open up the windows of heaven and pour you out a blessing that you will not have room enough to receive. With that being said, the question is, "What will you do when the windows of heaven is closed?" SHOUT! Why shout you say? You shout because though the windows may be closed, there may be and probably is a door opened elsewhere which could mean that the window wasn't large enough and/or maybe the place of blessing will not be large enough to fit through the window. It must come through the door!

THE WISDOM OF WITHDRAWAL

There are times, circumstances and events that will provoke one to withdraw. Some people see this as a negative, but there really is wisdom in withdrawing from matters that will provoke you to act in a manner that will bring reproach to the name of the one you represent. There is nothing wrong with removing yourself from people, circumstances and events, especially if it's in your best interest. I am one who hates to argue and I despise confrontation. I haven't always been that way because originally I was a fighter until God changed my nature. I learned the wisdom of withdrawal when I realized that the words that I speak, or the actions that I perform in anger cannot be undone when I cool off. As a matter of fact, even though I was a fighter I also realized that my words sting much longer than the blows that I threw in a fist fight. I learned that it is ok to take the high road and just withdraw and seek the face of the father on the matter and then retreat back to the situation in a spirit that bears fruit of the one that we represent.

Day 126

I'M STILL WORKING ON IT

Why is it that people shy away from showing their own humanity? Men feel like they have to exhibit the qualities of masculinity and machoism and women feel as though they have to be the damsel in distress. In Christendom, believers feel that they have arrived in some manner especially in the eyes of new converts or unbelievers. The true reality is that we all like to see and appreciate the humanity of everyone. There is greatness in the exhibition of your weakness. Let the world know that there are still some areas in your life in which you struggle. Stand firm in the reality that none of us are perfect. Live it, breathe it, show it, embrace it, but most of all share it because someone needs to see it.

Day 127

I STILL HAVE THE ABILITY TO LOVE!

Sometimes life can make us callous, cold and hard. It's not intentional, it's just when the heartbreak is frequent, sudden, or repetitive, we call ourselves protecting ourselves and building a wall around our emotions. What we don't realize is that the same barrier we use to protect ourselves, we also allow it to block the blessings of others and our ability to provide them with what we are called to offer them. Just because we have been used, abused and mistreated doesn't mean we have to return the favor to the universe. I know you're hurting, but you still have the ability to love. Someone needs you! I know you've been taken for granted but despite it all you still have the ability to love! Someone needs you! They needed you to experience that pain to help them through it. They needed you to experience that heartache to guide them through it. Someone needs you and your ability to love despite it all.

THE CARNAL CONCUBINE

<u>Carnal</u>- relating to or given to crude bodily pleasures and appetites

<u>Concubine</u>- a woman with whom a man cohabits without being married. They are recognized in society and in the household as less than a wife; mistress

I refuse to be the carnal concubine. The woman who expects no commitment from a man who says he loves me and plays the role of a mate but has not taken the bait of making me more than his date. The one who appreciates me for hips and dips and beautiful lips, but he won't listen to the words that come out of my mouth that shouts, "Pray for me!" "Fast with me!" "See me the way that Christ sees me!" "Love me like Christ loves the church!" I won't be treated like a beneficial piece of meat. These words I never want to repeat.

Day 129

THERE IS A WORSHIP IN YOUR WILDERNESS

As an avid intimate worshipper it is the only way that I get through adversity. The most important thing I had to understand was that my worship doesn't exempt me from adversity, but it is the vehicle that I use to help me get through the adversity that often seems to be too much for me to bear. The most significant thing about the wilderness experience is the fact that it is a place that God gets the full attention of his people. It is the location where intimacy takes place. The INTO-ME-SEE of worship is where the relationship between you and Christ are consummated. The deepest; most vulnerable place of your being is shown in the wilderness. Next time you see obstacles coming your way just worship! It works every time.

JUST WHEN..., THAT'S WHEN...

Just when I decided to follow Christ, that's when all hell broke loose. Just when I accepted my call, that's when my past came back to haunt me. Anytime you seek to advance in God, you better believe that there is going to be some opposition. Your "just when" experience always predicates the "that's when" opponent. Just when I thought I met the mate of my dreams, that's when I found out who they truly were. Just when I thought I had mastered this area in my life, that's when I got slapped back into the reality that I still have work to do. Don't get discouraged when "that's when" shows up, just stay the course of your "just when."

Day 131

HE WENT TO HIS GARDEN TO
HELP ME THROUGH MINE

The Garden of Gethsemane experience to me was one of the most humane acts of God. It was the place when even Jesus didn't want to be in the predicament that he was in. This place was the place where I really resonated with the issues that he went through. The fear, the betrayal, the fatigue, just to name a few of the emotions that I came to know and understand. In my most dire of needs, I always refer to this experience to get strength. It makes me feel as though I can really push past anything because he did it too.

If They were Meant to Stay, They Couldn't Leave!

Have you ever experienced the abandonment of people in your life? Have you ever been disappointed by their ability to just walk away when you felt like you needed them the most? Here is the great revelation of this matter, if they were meant to stay, they couldn't leave. By virtue of the fact that they are able to leave means that God never intended for them to stay in the first place. It's a hard pill to swallow, but it is the truth. If you chase them and make them stay, they will only block or maybe delay the blessings that are coming your way. Keeping people in your life beyond their expiration date will only bring spoilage to you harvest. Let them go and watch yourself grow!

THIS IS A PART OF THE PROCESS!

Life is all about process. Unfortunately, babies don't come out potty trained and walking. There is a such thing as developmentally appropriate. This means that everything and everyone must go through a process in order to be developed appropriately. Sometimes we are our own worst enemy. I know that for me personally I am super hard on myself to do things right and in the spirit of excellence, but for many years, and even sometimes now, I struggle with the concept that everything is a process. Process takes patience. This means keep your eye on the ultimate goal but at the same time don't expect to reach that ultimate goal overnight. Process also brings about purity. Pearls are extracted from a clam and the less like the others that they are, creates an additional value to the pearl itself. What am I trying to say you ask? All I am saying is that you are valuable to God and only he knows your expected end, the rest is all about your faith in him. Yes God gave you a vision of a thing that is to come, but whatever you do, hold on to that dream, don't lose focus and trust the process that he is taking you through to get to that vision.

Day 134

LOOK OUTSIDE THE BOX!

Religion is a limited form of God; it will cause you to look for his manifestation in a single way. You want financial increase pray for it and it will happen in God's timing they say. You want to be delivered, tarry at the alter with people hollering and screaming in your ear trying to drown out the voice of the enemy. You want to get over a bad relationship? Let us grease you down and turn you around in circles three times and shout Jesus to the top of your lungs and poof it will be done. NOT SO SAINTS!!! The reality is all of those things can be done in very simple ways. Seek God! God has a way of doing things that are so unconventional that it will amaze the human mind and understanding. So look outside of the box of the religious rhetoric and mentality and seek an authentic relationship with God and he will do all things well without the middle man.

Day 135

BREAK THE CONNECTION AND LOSE THE SUPPLY

Many times we are guilty of walking away from our divine connections and when we wonder why we lost the supply and provision that God has for us. It seems interesting that a few days ago we talked about letting them go and today we say don't cut off your supply. Here is the trick, and this is also where prayer and discernment come in. IF they were meant to stay, they couldn't leave, they wouldn't leave, but if they are called divinely in your life, then it's the responsibility of both parties to maintain that connection because when that connection is broken, then the supply of whatever is fueling the health of that relationship is lost.

PUT YOUR MOUTH ON IT

The Bible speaks clearly about the power of the tongue. There is life and death in the power of the tongue is a major one that comes to mind for the purpose of today's study. Whatever is in your life that you don't desire to have there, declare it dead! Whatever it is that you want more of in your life, speak life into it, and cause it to reproduce. This principle also speaks to the binding and loosing scripture. Whatsoever you bind on earth, shall be bound in heaven, and whatsoever you loose on earth, shall be loosed in heaven. So whatever you desire for the things of your life, put your mouth on it and watch God manifest what you said according to his riches in glory and his will and desire for your life.

GET TO THE LOWEST COMMON DENOMINATOR

In grade school, we are taught to that in order to add or subtract fractions we had to get to the lowest common denominator. Let's implement that same strategy in our spiritual lives. A fraction is the same symbol used for division and the revelation is that there are issues that we deal with in life that divides us within ourselves. This means that the elements of our being don't agree and are not on one accord, and for many people we walk around not in agreement in our inner beings. Our mind says one thing, and our heart says something else. Our spirit provokes us one way but our intellect leads us in the opposite direction. This is where we need to get down to the lowest common denominator so that addition can be made to our lives easier. This means we have to get to the root of our mess and clean it up, or pluck it out so that we can experience the increase that we desire. What is the root of your mess? Unforgiveness? Jealousy? The inability to release a past hurt or issue? Whatever it is, you have to make a conscious decision to get to the root of it, find its common denominator and then add or subtract it from your life.

THAT WAS MY PLAN!

Have you ever had a plan that was so picture perfect in your mind that it seemed as though it would be flawless and fool proof to execute? I have! Guess what happened! It was an epic fail, a royal disaster. Not every single time did it fail, but it happened enough for me to learn this lesson: yield my will to his and seek him first in all I do. There is an old cliché' that says, "Plans are made to be broken!" The revelation is that without a God consultation first your plans WILL be broken! The next time you seek to make a plan save yourself the trouble and consult God first and allow him to direct your path.

GOD, JUST BREATHE ON IT!

There are situations in all of our lives that seem to be lost, void, without life, and hopeless. It reminds me of the valley of dry bones where the questions was asked, "Can these dry bones live?" You may be asking the same questions about your situation. In my times of desperation my earnest cry is always that God would breathe on that thing and make it come to life. When I feel all hope is gone I ask, "God, just breathe on it!" When I feel as though I am out of options, my prayer is, "God, just breathe on it!" When I don't know which way to turn, I cry out, "God, just breathe on it!" Breathe on my mind, body, soul and spirit and yes even my intellect when I think that I have it all figured out "God, just breathe on it!"

So You Want to Be Me?

Many people look at my life and my achievements and accolades. They look at the books, the cds, degress, career, children, grandchildren and the like and say that I make it look so easy which results in the famous phrase, "I want to be like you!" My response is always, "Are you sure?" "Can I tell you...?" "It ain't easy because..." I try to live my life very transparently to enable people to see not only my ups, but also my downs. This is a two sided approach to my success. On one hand, people love and appreciate my honesty and truth in which I walk in daily, but then there are the others who try to use my past against me. Both of these sides of the coin play a very significant part in my success. Why? Because they both motivate me to continue to live my best life and my fullest truth to the best of my ability and at the end of the day I only want God to be seen and glorified in my life for it is only through him that I can do all things.

Day 141

I Got Someone Living With Me

It is statistically proven that the elderly live longer when they have something living with them. It doesn't specify what, but it just says something living with them. It can be a cat, a dog, a fish or a plant. Believers need the Lord living with them. This is important so that when people see you going through your storms, they need to see that you have something, someone living with you. First of all, you have God, the father, God, the son, and God the Holy Spirit, but more so, you have the twins grace and mercy following you all the days of your life. So take your posse and step out on the measure of faith that you have and make it do what it do!

THE DÉJÀ VU OF DISTRACTION

Isn't it interesting that every time you seek after God intensely, a distraction comes. Why? This is the question that I have been wrestling with for most of my life. Then wisdom stepped in and said, "Its Déjà vu silly!" See when we go through things and they happen repetitively, it seems that we are going through the same thing over and over again. Its Déjà vu! Déjà vu, from French, literally means "already seen", is the phenomenon of having the strong sensation that an event or experience currently being experienced has already been experienced in the past. Déjà vu is a feeling of familiarity, and déjà vécu (the feeling of having "already lived through" something) is a feeling of recollection. Either way, the point of the matter is to learn from it finally, and mature to a point where you expect it and never yield to it. Live, love, learn and do better.

Day 143

I Didn't Forget, I Choose not to Remember

We often hear that we should forgive and forget. However, there are sometimes in life where we forgive, but we can't forget. That is the time when I make a choice to choose not to remember. See all things in life are a learning experience and in that experience comes maturity. When you are mature, you are able to see things as a learning curve. You experienced it, you lived through it, and you can help someone else along the way. There are also times that we just have to trust our actions. As a single woman in the scene of dating, I would encounter a lot of men. Of course you do the traditional exchanging of the numbers and all that jazz. There would come a point where I would stop talking to the individual for whatever reason and then they would just pop up as if nothing happened. When asked, "Can we start over?" My answer would always be, "No, because if you were someone that I felt compelled to relate with, then I would have stayed in contact!" It doesn't matter how long it had been and how much they said they had changed, I would always be compelled to trust my actions to not pursue anything further with them. So trust yourself and choose not to remember the former things, but press on into the purpose and path that God has for you!

THERE IS ALWAYS ANOTHER

My favorite apostle in the Bible was the Apostle Paul, well actually he and Peter, and the reason is because I can relate to them both. Many people call me the female version of Peter because I am normally the one to say what everyone else is thinking, but just aren't bold enough to say. Then I am likened to Peter for his transparency. This is especially true in the truth he spoke when he said, "I count not myself to have apprehended, but this one thing I do is I am forgetting those things which are behind me and I press towards the mark for the prize of the high calling which is in Christ Jesus." I love this because it is a scripture that remains relevant in the lives of everyone forever and always. See, we never master this thing we call "life" because as we master one thing, there is always another thing that we must encounter and overcome to get one step closer to the prize of the high calling. This is a great fact because it keeps us humble and completely dependent on Christ.

THERE IS A PROCESS TO YOUR PURPOSE

I'm reminded of a time when my children were smaller and there was a stroller that I wanted soooo bad because it was perfect for both of them to ride in though they were two different sizes. I worked hard to get the money for that stroller, mind you I was 18 years old and they had just come out with these strollers so they were expensive. So I finally got enough money to get one and I was so excited. I couldn't wait to get home and open the box and put my babies in it and go for many walks. Then I opened the box and saw the million and one pieces that was in the box. Now I knew what it was supposed to look like in the end but it didn't look nothing like it when I took it out of the box. As a much older and wiser person now, I get the revelation of it all. See only God knows what we will look like in the end and what we see right now in ourselves are the million and one pieces that I saw in the box. The beauty of life is when we are being put together piece by piece. There is a process that we must go through in order for us to be polished for our purpose. Whether the pieces were in a million pieces in a box or put together to make this phenomenal stroller that I just paid a lot of money for, it was still a stroller. You are still who God called you to be whether you are in a million pieces or all together, you will forever be in the process for your purpose.

THE FIGHT BETWEEN WHAT YOU HEARD
AND WHAT GOD TOLD YOU

As a child I was abused and for years my mother would tell me how ugly I was and how I wasn't going to ever be anything more than a pretty face to anyone. Everything that I did, I succeeded at and yet she never really told me that she was proud of me and for years and years; even after her death I would do things to get her approval. My other book, "And Deliver Us from People" was all about this part of my life and how I got over it. Nevertheless, before God dealt with me on this issue I always wrestled with what I heard her tell me for many years of my life and what I heard God say to and about me. My faith wanted to believe him who I had never seen, but the voice of my mother would always drown out the promises that God made me concerning my life. I wish I could tell you that to this day I don't still struggle with this from time to time, but that would be a lie. However I know now that the fight between what I heard and what God told me is already fixed and in the end and even now I WIN because his name is above all names and he's worthy of all our praise. Walk in your victory and realize that his words are all that matter. If no one tells you they are proud of you know that I am and so is God. No matter what anyone else has to say, whether they support you or not, listen to what God has to say to you.

THE SPEED LIMITS OF LIFE

In these times that we are living in and everything is so instantaneous, we have forgotten how to slow down and enjoy the moment. When is the last time you went to an event and no one pulled out a phone to video tape something or to take a selfie or the like? It is my fear that we are all breaking the speed limits of life. We are rushing to go here and running to go there and never enjoying the process of getting there, nor do we live in the moment when we are there. The old people used to always say, "Take the time to smell the flowers!" I now understand what they meant and I challenge you today to take a moment to just live and be present in the moment and thank God for that moment before getting to the point where you are forced to slow down and enjoy it. Enjoy it by choice.

YOU DON'T HAVE TO STAY WHERE YOU STARTED

I don't care where you came from; I don't care what you have been through YOU DON'T HAVE TO STAY THERE. Moving on is a choice that must be made by the individual who will take responsibility for their own destiny. I made up in my mind a long time ago that I wanted to be someone and I wanted to do things that have never been in my family. Not only did I make this vow, but I have some cousins who made the same vow. I have a great family and we have all walked very different paths, but at the end of the day it is always a joy to sit back and watch us all surpass our parents and want more than what they had. It is a joy to see and it makes my heart glad to know that we all have the same mentality that we will not stay where we started, but we will create a new path for our generation and the generations thereafter us. #Greater works shall you do!

Day 149

I GOT A SCREAM IN ME!

Have you ever been so blown away by what God is doing that all you could do was stand there like the kid in the movie "Home Alone". Holding your face together with your hands because it is just so mind boggling that you are too shocked to share, too grateful to second guess? Those are the times when I just find me a field, a track or some outside edifice where I can just stand and scream to the top of my lungs how great God is and people won't think I'm crazy or being beaten in my home. Now watch this, it's not only in the times that he does something that I get this screaming unction, but just at times when I think about all that I have been through. I just have to give it up to him because he and he alone is worthy!

I'm a Gift to You

As a child of the Most high, I think that we at times forget just how valuable we are. Businesses stay open because of the favor on our life. Relationships stay connected because of the cohesive anointing on our lives. Marriages survive because of our prayers. Our country has survived on the shoulders of the believers. With this reality being spelled out, I think that we can confidently say to ones who seem to forget our value in their lives, "I am a gift to you!" When we enter into relationships with others, I think it is only fitting that we kindly remind them, "I am a gift to you!" Not only that but it also serves as a reminder to us just how important we are to each other. Come on; as you go out today and you encounter opposition just stop the individual in their tracks and say, "I am a gift to you!"

I'M GOING AGAINST THE GRAIN

You know you're talking to God when it doesn't make any sense to you. You know that you are in the will of God when you rub others the wrong way. When you are a minority in the world, you are probably the majority with Christ. I always get worried when I enter into a place where I am doing what everyone else is doing. It's just not in my make up to be normal, ordinary, and the go with the flow kind of girl. My grandmother would call it "the road that is less traveled" is where I reside. So look around, do you look like the crowd, or are you on a cloud all alone. Remember you are called to be different, separated, set aside, and called out for such a time as this.

THESE HANDS

These hands have been through some things that my mouth may never tell,

These hands have been through some things that my mind cannot conceptualize

These same hands that can hurt, has chosen to be used to heal instead

These hands never do anything without consulting the head.

These hands have transitioned from fighting flesh and blood

To wrestling with wisdom with principalities.

These hands rise in worship,

These hands clap in praise,

These hands create sounds of thunder,

The power in these hands have left many to wonder:

Who? How? When? Where?

The transformation of these hands make me say to you, you just had to be there.

ONLY FOR YOU LORD

I do what I do for you lord, no one else. Anyone who knows me knows that I am a worshipper from my heart. When I was considering joining a church, the Pastor asked me what is it that I can't live without and my response was "Worship." Some might think it strange that as a mother I didn't say my children or my mate or my grandchildren and I too was initially surprised at my response. It was an immediate download from the Holy Ghost and of course I had to follow up on my response. See before there were children, grandchildren and spouses there was God. Whenever I go through anything I always find consolation in my worship. When I am worshipping it's like there is no one in the room but me and God. It's my time of consummation with him. It's the time when I see myself giving back to him what he has given to me and I just happen to include others in the room in on it. Most praise and worship leaders lead an aerobic experience for the congregation and hope God is pleased along the way. I, on the other hand, perform for an audience of one. Only for you Lord!

ROCK STEADY BABY

One of my favorite artist is Aretha Franklin and she has a song called, "Rock Steady Baby" many of you may know it. The lyrics are nowhere near spiritual, but the title is what I want to draw attention to. See when we are going through our issues in life and the boat of survival that we are on seems to be rocking violently, the message is to just rock steady. Yes, the storms may come, the tides may rise and the winds may blow, but whatever you do, don't fall off the boat. Find the groove of the storm and rock steady. That means don't lose your balance, hold on for dear life and rock steady baby. Yes you may have to cry and you may stumble and you may even fall, but get up and rock steady baby. Know that all things are working together for your good and that no weapon formed against you shall prosper so JUST ROCK STEADY!

Day 155

DON'T SAY NOTHING

There are times when we are going through so much adversity that we get lost in our thoughts and we don't know the words to say. Thank God that he sees and knows all and most of all thank God for the Holy Ghost who will intercede on our behalf when words fall short of articulating the pain that we are experiencing. There are times when you need to know that it is ok to just say nothing. God knows your hurts; you don't have to say nothing! He knows your innermost pains; you don't have to say nothing! He knows your wants; you don't have to say nothing! He also knows you needs, you don't have to say nothing! Just know that there is a time when you can't say anything. As I was writing this book, God had me on a fast and he told me strategically what to do and during some of the fast I would find myself just lying in bed doing absolutely nothing just enjoying the peace and presence of the Lord and I didn't want, need, or have to say a word, but I knew he had it all worked out.

REBUKE OR RELATIONSHIP

I remember when I was younger, the first time that I got rebuked publicly. I thought that it was the most humiliating and disrespectful thing that a person could go through. I didn't even feel better that I was not alone in my rebuke. I never took it personal, because I knew that God chastens those that he loves. Needless to say I hurried up and got that thing right; however it did cause me to reflect on the experience often. See many people get upset when they are rebuked or chastised and often find themselves leaving the church in anger and crying "church hurt." I think the biggest factor for leaders is that we must establish a relationship with the person first and let them grow and mature under our tutelage. I don't believe that the Lord would have you to rebuke anyone without that prior relationship because they are not sure where your motive is. The trick in that is that you want to make sure also that the rebuke is not critical of the person, but of the spirit in which the rebuke is against. All of this comes with teaching and maturation in the body of Christ. My advice to the readers of today's devotional is that we must be able to enter into relationship and accept rebuke and understand that it has nothing to do with the person to person relationship, but the spiritual relationship between you and Christ.

I'm Out

We as believers have to learn when to walk away, when to say, "I'm Out!" My Pastor teaches us all the time about the need to have personal core values in which you live by and how those core values often come from your pain and experience. He went on to teach us that anytime we encounter a person or experience that puts those core values in jeopardy, its ok to say "I'm Out!" My core values are loyalty, honesty, integrity, accountability, transparency and humility. Anytime I encounter someone or something that does not operate in those core values, I have no problem saying, "I'm Out!" This goes for personal, professional, family, or friend relationships. I have a spirit in me that is called the "I'm Out!" spirit. For the longest time I wouldn't use it because I know what it feels like to be left and abandoned, but when I found my voice, I gave myself permission to remain loyal enough to be true to myself and my core values and therefore now I have no problem saying, "I'm Out!"

It Should've been Me

I learned at an early age not to judge people for the things that they go through especially when it comes to criminal activity. There was a time in my life that I was a big time fighter because I was being abused and could not nor would not tell anyone. My only alternative was to keep it bottled up inside and after a while I would find myself lashing out at others, especially people that I didn't know because then there was no reason for remorse. So when I go and minister at prisons with violent criminals, I always share my story and tell them that I love them because I should be them, but it's only by the grace of God that I'm not. How many people can relate to others on that level and are transparent enough to share their hurts, their pains and their struggles. This is part of the reason that I believe that I am half as successful as I am because of the fact that I am transparent, honest and relatable. Count it not robbery to share your story with others because it lets them see the hope of the Lord. IT lets them see that there is another side to their situation if they just remain humble and true and hold themselves accountable.

THE BALANCE OF SELFISHNESS AND SELFLESSNESS

Some people will try to make you feel bad when you take care of yourself. I know whenever I would enter into relationships; I would always hear the other person tell me how spoiled I was. After a while it actually became offensive. Then I went through a phase of proving to others that I was not spoiled so I would give everything that I had to others, whether they appreciated it or not, and I wouldn't dare tell someone "No." That took me to a point of burnout and exhaustion. After a while God matured me to the point of understanding that there is a balance between selfishness and selflessness. I am not spoiled, but I am blessed beyond measure. When the scripture talks about my cup overfloweth. He showed me that everything in the cup is for you/me, as an individual, and the overflow is for others. So if that means that the less mature calls me spoiled, then that is an opportunity to share my revelation with them and hopefully get them to see the same principle. We have to be able to care for ourselves before we can care for others which is why on the airplane the stewardess always says that in the case of an emergency, place the mask on yourself FIRST and then help others. So it is in the spiritual realm.

REJECTION FOR AFFECTION

Do you know how it feels to be rejected? Rejection comes in many forms, and no matter the form the pain is all the same. I used to let the rejection fester inside of me and make me bitter, but then when I took the time to reflect on the occurrences of my rejection one day, I saw a vision and in that vision there was myself, God and a person. The person had no face, so naturally I couldn't make out who the person was, but I saw them consistently rejecting me. I saw myself sitting there crying and then God would be standing right there and I would just sit in front of him and I never ran to him for consolation. I woke up with tears that had soaked my pillows. I felt so horrible and lower than dirt. Then when I returned to sleep I had the same vision, except this time I watched a reenactment of my favorite event in the Bible which is when Jesus went to the Garden of Gethsemane and I saw how he handled the rejection, where he retreated to his father for consolation. That was his way of showing me how to handle the rejections in my life. Now I exchange my earthly rejection for God's affection.

Day 161

GUILTY OR INNOCENT

I am a fan of crime shows, some of them anyway, and I have always wondered how attorneys could represent someone guilty of the horrible crimes that they committed. Then I thought about the way that Christ loves us, whether we are guilty or innocent. I used to look down on the attorneys until I got that revelation because Christ knows that we are guilty, but yet he still loves us and advocates for us. He stands in the gap and intercedes on our behalf as an advocate to the father. This is the ultimate sacrifice and love that he can show us. I am not saying that the lawyers are correct in their convictions, but what I will say is that if I were one I would definitely have to keep this analogy in mind as I do my job. So the next time that you see someone who has offended you, take a moment and think of this analogy and understand that you had to be forgiven and they (whoever has offended you) deserve that same measure of love.

KEEP IT MOVING

This is not the time to stand still, but to move and see the salvation of the Lord. For too long we have cried and whined about how we went through this and we went through that. It is now time to move on from the things that are of the former days, and let's just look forward to the days to come. I promise you our latter will be greater than our former because the word tells us so. Let's make our next days, our best days. Listen, what can you really do about the days that are gone? Nothing right? Just learn from them and keep it moving. Yes, they lied on you, but keep it moving! Yes, they stabbed you in your back, but keep it moving! Yes, you were misunderstood, but keep it moving! Whatever you do JUST KEEP IT MOVING!

YOU LOVE ME WHY?

Due to the days of my past, I used to always find myself asking people why it is that they loved me. I was so used to people loving me for what I could do for them and all other reason. Rarely did I find anyone who loved me simply because of me. It took me a long time to get over that, but when I did it freed me up to see that people can actually love me authentically. When I got the revelation of this truth, I set boundaries when I saw otherwise and never hesitated to release them from my life and my presence.

PROFOUND, BUT NOT COMPLETE

I don't know about you, but I get super excited when I get a word from the Lord. When I get one it's not always about what I am getting, but it is about the fact that out of the millions and billions of people on the earth, that he thought enough of me to send me a word. As a prophetess myself, I am always sure to share the prophetic word with the person, and I always ensure that they get the entire word. Sometimes the word can be so profound that it provokes an emotion in them that has them screaming and hollering and, often times, when this happens they miss the instruction that goes along with the prophecy. So the word is profound and promising, but not complete, and then they wonder why it is that they have not received the promise and it goes back to the fact they did not receive the instruction that was needed for them get to the promise. Don't get so caught up on the profound that you forget to get the complete word.

HOW DOES GOD SEE ME

I used to place a lot of value on how people viewed me and their opinion of me. It didn't take long before I grew out of that phase. In fact, I wrote an entire book about that process and what it looked like. That book was written in seven days, and it outlined the process of me killing the people pleaser within me. We all have that person inside of us that longs to get the approval of others. With that being said, there comes a time in all of our lives that we will mature and only worry about the approval of God. The assurance of his love and view of us will be all that matters. The great thing about that truth is that God's view of us never changes. He loves us with an undying love.

I DON'T KNOW HOW TO RECEIVE IT

Many times God wants to bless us, but we block it with this thing called pride. I know for one, I have always been one who was afraid to ask people for help with anything because I was afraid that I would have to hear it again. As I have lived and learned, I see that my fear is oftentimes, a reality. There is also a reality that there are some really good people out there that want to help you out in any way possible, and your negative experience with one person should not force you to try to abort the blessing of someone who authentically wants to help you. Now the next time someone offers you assistance, just be honest and tell them, I don't know how to receive it. There is a blessing attached to the people who want to bless you and when you deny them the ability to help you, you are not only blocking your blessing, but their blessing as well. Ask God to help you to receive the blessings that he is trying to give to you through the hands of others.

I'm Informed on Another Level, I Can't Expect You to Understand

Many times we expect people to see things from our perspective when clearly they don't have the connection nor the relationship with Christ that we have. I remember one time I was talking to someone, and I was really into the conversation. I was just talking a mile a minute about a matter that I was really passionate about. When I took a breath to ask them why they were looking at me like that their response was, "I have no idea what you are talking about." Now I thought that I was speaking plain English that any and everybody could understand, but clearly I was wrong. Or better yet, how many times as parents, or adults in general, have we told a kid about behaviors that they didn't think that we knew about and their response was, "How did you know that?" This happens all the time. The answer is clear! We, as believers, are informed on a whole other level than the natural man. We have to be cognizant of this fact as we encounter others and make sure that we don't place an unrealistic expectation on them to understand matters that they can't comprehend because they are not informed on that level, especially if they do not have the Holy Ghost. He is our ultimate informer, and the revealer of all truths, even the truths that others are trying to hide.

IF I CAN JUST GET IT IN MY SPIRIT

If I can get it in my spirit, it's just a matter of time before I get it in my life. As believers, there are layers to our being, and each layer must be penetrated with authentic truths that permeates through the prior untruths that we have been told. The truth of the matter is that many times when we are told a thing, especially if it is out of our comfort zone or out of the ordinary of what we have been told. When a word penetrates our ears it also gets into our spirit. Our spirit should be the driving force to our being, therefore if you want to get your mind to do a thing; it must first be dropped into your spirit, even and especially, if it can't be conceptualized in your mind. Whatever you are believing God for, just get it in your spirit and allow that to be the driving force for your decisions and even more so your actions.

Day 169

NO MORE FEAR, STRETCH FORTH YOUR HAND

Mark 3:5

Beyond where you are is where you need to reach. It hurts to stretch! But Stretch forth your hand. It's scary to stretch! But stretch forth your hand. I know you're tired! But stretch forth your hand. I know you're frustrated! But stretch forth your hand. They have plucked your last nerve and you are ready to throw in the towel, but whatever you do, DON'T GIVE UP! Stretch forth your hand. What do I mean when I say stretch forth thy hand? I mean extend your hands in worship. Release everything that is bothering you there at his feet. Give him your hurt, your pain, your frustration, all things that have you bound, just give it to him and know that he and he alone, can handle it without your assistance. No matter what it looks like or how it feels just stretch forth your hand.

IT'S TIME TO TURN THE PAGE!

Many people in your life will judge, and to be honest sometimes we judge ourselves based on the prior pages of our life story. I know, I for one, have made a number of mistakes and I can be my own worst enemy. But what I realized is that I had to be the first one in my life to turn the page. Meaning, start anew and afresh. Give myself a break, a fresh start and a new beginning. When I embraced this opportunity, I released myself from a lot of baggage, guilt, hurt and shame. Now I want to pass this same strength to you and encourage you to turn the page in your life. Stop living in the same chapter over and over. It's over, it's done, it is finished now turn the page, and anyone who wants to bring up your past serve them notice that you have turned the page in your life.

MEET HIM AT THE WELL

Many of us know the story about the woman at the well. She was one who was at a place getting one thing that she perceived she needed, and wind up getting something that was made evident that she needed. She went to get water, which was her perceived need, but she wound up getting a word from the Lord himself which was evident. Many people go to church with their own agenda, be it a tradition, an expectation or a ritual, but at the end of the day the hope is that everyone leaves there with much more. I love when I go to church because I liken myself to the woman at the well in so many ways. The well is a place where I go to be refilled and restored. It is a place where I can make a divine appointment with God and he and I can have our time together. I am in a corporate setting to where he is able to use others to speak for him and/or to confirm a word that he has already given me in our private time together. I dare you today to make an appointment with the father and tell him exactly what you need. Meet him at the well and be restored.

RUN? OR PATIENCE?

The scripture tells us to lay aside every weight so we can RUN with PATIENCE this race. It seems to be a bit of a contradiction because how can one run and be patient at the same time? How can someone move and be still? How can someone live, but yet die? This is the oxymoron of faith. You know what your needs are, you know what the promises of God are over your life, and you know him to be faithful to his promises, so what do you do in the meantime? You wait! Not only do you wait, but you keep moving, keep living, keep breathing, keep believing, and be patient. Die to your faith daily. Force the members of your being to yield to the will of the Lord and watch God work.

IT'S OUR FAULT

When will we, as leaders, take responsibility for the fact that the congregation is filled with mimics and clones of one another? Why is this infection running ramped among us? The reason is because leaders are not meeting the needs of the people to help them put the puzzle pieces of their individuality together. Someone's ego is being stroked because they look amongst their congregation and see a lot of mirror images. Have you ever met a potential mate and asked them the hard questions of who it is they look up to or that they admire? Ask to meet that person? Upon meeting that person or googling that person if it is a public figure, see if those individuals resemble each other in any way. If so beware there may be an identity crisis occurring. With all of the books that there are out there, it would seem that this issue would decrease in popularity, but the sad part is many people won't read, and if they do read, they don't apply what they read. I believe that as leaders it is up to us to teach people how to be individuals and to walk in their own shoes and tell their own story. It's ok to emulate someone, but imitation to me is the lowest form of flattery, JUST BE YOU!

Day 174

THE POWER OF I'M SORRY

There are a number of people who have offended us over the span of our lifetimes. The sad thing is that many won't ever come back and apologize for their actions. The question is, "How will you handle that reality?" Many people say, "Forgive and forget" others say, "Just let it go." The truth of the matter is, and I know that you all have heard it before; unforgiveness hurts no one but you. I know the power of unforgiveness on your health and your sanity and I promise you it is not worth it. I know firsthand. Unforgiveness is cancer of the soul. The reason that I entitled this devotional the "Power of I'm Sorry" is because I have seen, first hand, the Power of I'm Sorry, even when it doesn't come from the one who offended you. I was unchurched at one time because a Pastor had hurt me to my core. Upon the request of a friend, I visited her church a few times and I really loved it. One Sunday after a powerful sermon that Pastor, who had no idea who I was and what I was going through, extended an alter call and he said, "I know that someone in here has been hurt deeply and please allow me to apologize on behalf of that person. The thing that they did was wrong and uncalled for and the apology that you deserve, you will never get from them so let me do it." I was completely blown away, but that apology changed my life forever. To this day I still love and respect that pastor, and he will always be like a father to me. He showed me the power of I'm Sorry.

347

THAT'S WHERE I WAS, THAT'S NOT WHERE I AM

I am one who believes in longevity of relationships, but the issue with that is the fact that though you may transcend from one place to another, the friendship may not. One of the hardest things to do in life is to release a relationship that you personally value. The interesting thing is when you watch it all unfold or reflect back on the relationship only to see that those people are often the ones who are not able to see and celebrate where you are because they can't see past where you have been. I call it still living at my old address. This can be poisonous and detrimental to your own success which is why, often, these people are the ones whom God will sever the ties in order to elevate you. So don't cry over where you have been and who you have been with, but embrace where you are going and celebrate the ones who are able to accompany you.

IGNORANCE IS A CHOICE

Though many fail to realize it or they operate in denial. Ignorance is definitely a choice. You make decisions even when you choose not to. When it comes time to vote on the matters of our nation, if you choose to vote or not to vote, you still made a decision. When you choose not to vote, you are subliminally saying, "I will just go with majority." This takes away your rights to complain. In the days of the internet and the World Wide Web, you can research and look up absolutely anything that you need and/ or want to know. From biblical matters, to politics, to even educational endeavors and opportunities it is all at your fingertips. When it comes to matters of Christendom, the same opportunities apply. Almost all churches have some form of church school, be it Bible Study and/or church school or Sunday School as they called it in the days of old. With that being said, when you choose not to attend, you are in reality choosing to be ignorant to Satan's tactics and devices, and even more so the promises of God. I was called to preach at a very young age, and I was raised as a Baptist preacher, then as we began to move around with the military, we went overseas and joined an evangelical church. By the time I was 18, my mother had went through a season of taking us to whatever church had the best choir. By the time she died, we were members of an A.M.E. (African Methodist Episcopal) Church. With all those different doctrines, beliefs, and creeds, I chose not to be ignorant so I went to a nondenominational seminary school and acquired my PH.D. In this school, we were made to live an assigned amount of time in each religion and denomination and to do extensive research. This made me stronger as a believer and more convicted in my faith in him. From that experience, many would think that I would not still attend church education settings, but in reality it became my passion and has led me to become more involved in the education of people when it comes to Christendom. Why? Because I am ever learning and I realize that ignorance is a choice and I CHOOSE not to be ignorant.

Day 177

THE WOUNDED WINNER

Though I have been wounded, I am a winner! How can I declare victory with my limbs hanging on a thread? I can declare victory because I made it. I can declare victory because I did not bend nor break. I can declare victory because, though I may be wounded, time can heal all wounds. I still have my life. I still have my strength. I still have the activity of my limbs. I still have the ability to tell my story. I can still help someone else along the way. I may be wounded, but I am a winner. I may be battered, but I am a winner. I may have lost some of the battles, but the war was fixed and the victory is mine. How? I'm glad you asked! It is because I am a child of the most High God who can do any and all things, but fail.

WARNING, WARNING

Luke 22:31, 32
³¹ And the Lord said, Simon, Simon, behold, Satan hath desired to have you, that he may sift you as wheat:
³² But I have prayed for thee, that thy faith fail not: and when thou art converted, strengthen thy brethren.

No matter what we go through the Lord will never leave us ignorant, nor unprepared for an attack. As we see in the scripture above. Though Peter was one of the most flawed of his disciples, Jesus still ensured that he was prepared for the attacks of the enemy. The issues are that when warnings come, what will we do? Will we heed them, or will we ignore them? The problem is that many of us ignore them, and then we get mad at God when we feel blindsided.

THE 3 S FOR KINGDOM SUCCESS

1 Peter 5:8-10

Strategy---[8] Be sober (showing self-control), be vigilant (alert); because your adversary the devil, as a roaring lion, walketh about, seeking whom he may devour (consume destructively):

Security----[9] Whom resist steadfast in the faith, knowing that the same afflictions are accomplished in your brethren that are in the world.

Solidarity---[10] But the God of all grace, who hath called us unto his eternal glory by Christ Jesus, after that ye have suffered a while, make you perfect, stablish, strengthen, settle you.

In every war, or every game, there is always a strategy and/or a game plan. The Kingdom of God is no different. There are the three S words for Kingdom success and especially when it comes to warfare. First of all, you have to have a strategy to complete the task. You know the enemy is going to come, so be prepared. As you prepare, don't be scared, but walk in the security that the fight is fixed and you won. God even made a way for your repair and recovery from the storm. This is why I serve the God I do!

Day 180

I'M STILL HERE

Broken, but I'm still here
Wounded, but I'm still here
Hurting, but I'm still here
Doubting, but I'm still here
No matter what I go through, I am blessed and highly encouraged
because I am still here.

THE AGGRAVATION OF WANT, AND THE ELEVATION OF NEED

Romans 7
Galatians 5

Many would believe the common misconception that once you get saved everything is fine and that you go on to live this life that is no longer filled with the events of your former days. We make the mistake of telling people come to Jesus, and everything will be alright and though this saying is partially true, there is still a processing that must take place in the life of every new creature that does not feel good, but it's good for you. Now in the middle of your processing, there are new revelations that should be happening and in the midst of it all. There is a silent war going on that if the matters of your mind are not fully persuaded, one will give in and though you think you have won the battle, in the midst of it all, you have lost the war! What do you mean Jennifer, I'm glad you asked! I am saying that this particular passage of scripture is telling us that the war is between our flesh and our spirit man....this is an ongoing thing that is a lifelong encounter with struggle. The variance comes in the small battles that make up the full experience of the war! Ok, let me come to your street ladies, you see Lola's husband down the street, yeah you see the wedding band, and you know his wife well, but every time you look at him, body parts that haven't moved in a long time begin to turn. That is the battle because your members say to approach him, but your mind says, "Girl, now you know he's married (further the illustration)...you WANT him because your sexually frustrated, but you NEED to leave him alone and consecrate yourself for the elevation of getting your own man. Come on somebody! So there is always a battle going on and let's be real, there are some battles that you will lose, but it does not mean that you lost the war.

RENEWAL

Romans 12 1-3

"Renewing" This word alludes to the fact that transformation is not a one hit wonder. This thing has to be done, for some daily, but for the short bus people like me it has to be done by the minute. Excuse me, I mean the second because I can feel the frustration of my want but I see the elevation of my need. This is why I can't be moved by people's feelings, because the frustration comes in us when our wants and needs don't line up. For many of us who have ever suffered from any mental issues, be it depression, bipolar disorder, narcissism, or anything of this nature, it is because we have allowed this frustration to consume us and have not sought God for the revelation of the situation. We have not spent enough time with God and talking to him and watch this, LISTENING TO HIM! To see how he feels about the situation. Seek him today, and see what he has to say about the matters that have been keeping you up at night, making you stay on the verge of tears when you try to be strong. I dare you to ask him to renew you and your thoughts.

THE CRITICAL NATURE OF MY CAVE EXPERIENCE

Did you ever think about the fact that when a person enters the intensive care unit in a hospital that there are restrictions on visitors and the like that the patients on the regular floor don't get. Have you ever wondered why? I have, and here is the revelation of it. See when you enter the intensive care unit, there is an extra level or layer of care that is made available to you and you are in a more critical state. Sometimes you may even be bumped up a level to the critical care unit, which is even more restrictive. The reason why is because they are trying to keep the contaminates that you are exposed to down, and they are also there to ensure that they are able to get to you at a moment's notice, if anything happens. There comes a point when we have to retreat to a cave to find refuge from the natural disasters of life. It is critical when this takes place because that is when God is trying to protect you from the contaminants not of your flesh, but of your spirit man. That cave becomes your intensive care unit and can mean life or death to your spirit man.

WITH MATURITY CAME LIBERTY

There is a level of liberty and freedom that comes with spiritual maturity. Many of us who have grown up in the church have experienced the bondage of religion and tradition. We done things that we had no idea why we did it, it was just because it was a thing that had always been done. Those methods had no biblical credence at all, it was just a tradition. However, the more mature that you become in Christ, the more that you develop in your relationship with him and it becomes more personal and you will shed away the weight of tradition and can operate more freely because we know who we serve, how to serve and more so, why we serve. This is not only when maturity has arrived, but also when the scripture of whom the son sets free is free indeed comes to mind and is revealed.

YES, I'M THIRSTY

The world has taken a biblical term and given it a negative connotation. In the world, the term "thirsty" means that one is in need of something in excess that they themselves can attain, but they choose to use others to get it, especially in relationships. But in the spiritual realm it means to have a need or desire for God that only he can fill. So, yes I am thirsty! I am thirsty for his touch! I am thirsty for his anointing! I am thirsting for all that he has for me. I am thirsty for a real and right relationship with him. I am thirsty to see the manifestation of his glory in all that I do. Yes, I am thirsty, how about you?

Day 186

NEVER ALONE, EVEN WHEN YOU'RE LONELY

There is big difference in being alone and being lonely. To be lonely is a state of mind, when you feel lost and a sense of abandonment. To be alone is a physical aspect of not having any type of companionship. Though many of us go through our lonely phases, we have to remember that we are never alone. Jesus promised that he would never leave us nor forsake us. He promised that he would be there til the end of time. Though our state is lonely, we always have a companion in Christ. Though it may not fill that earthly void, when we keep our minds on the things of Christ, we realize that loneliness is just that a state of mind, but also it is also an avenue for the enemy to creep in and begin to play with your mind and emotions and tell us all manners of evil to get us involved in our feelings and emotions. Rebuke him immediately, and force him to flee. Cover yourself, your mind, and your emotions in the blood of Jesus, and remember you are never alone.

THE PRESSURE COOKER

I have always marveled at the manner in which food cooks in the pressure cooker. The meat comes out so much more tender, and the seasoning is just right. When I looked at it from a spiritual standpoint, it all made sense. Food cooks well in the pressure cooker because it is isolated. There are not a lot of other foods in the same heat. It is also more tender because it is under extreme pressure to come out the best that it can be. The seasoning is correct because it stews in its own juices. What does this mean? It means that life experience is the pressure cooker, you are the entrée, and your reaction is the pressure. Life experience will sometimes force you to isolate yourself; there are not many others around. The pressure will extract the best out of you and the anointing and love of God are the juices that you are forced to marinate in, which allows one to come out tender to the needs of the people that you encounter. So don't curse the pressure cooker because you will come out the better for having been pressurized.

DON'T BE THAT LEAK!

Leaky people hurt people. Who are leaky people? I am glad you asked. Leaky people are the ones who speak out of time and season. They take the hidden things about others and themselves that God has shown them and they share it prematurely to seem spiritually deep and important. These are the ones who God says that he cannot trust them with his treasures. See time and season are everything in God. Even Jesus did not reveal himself or operate before his time because he knew the detriment of moving prematurely. It's like giving a car to a five-year-old old and allowing him or her to drive. It is physically impossible for them to handle the task, one because of their size; they can't see over the wheel AND touch the pedal at the same time. Cognitively, they are not developmentally able to multitask in that manner. This is why you cannot reveal the things of God to a babe too soon. They will take and run with it and try to operate out of their ignorance and do more damage than good. When you are shown something by God, pray about it and ask him why he showed it to you and the next plan of action to take.

Day 189

THE ANOINTING IS ON THE OBEDIENCE

When you understand that the only way to operate in your spiritual gifts is under the unction of the anointing, it is normal to desire the anointing of God over your life. It is critical to understand that the anointing comes through your obedience and through spending time with him. It is also critical to understand that it is the anointing that destroys the yoke, and to operate without it renders you ineffective. Yes, anyone can get up to sing a song in praise and worship, but what makes the difference is when the anointing steps in and takes the worship experience from an ordinary melodic performance, to one that is life changing and that transcends from an individual effort to a corporate experience that all can benefit from. So as your chasing after God, be sure to seek after his anointing over your life. Whatever he tells you to do, be sure to do it to ensure that the anointing is granted in exchange for your obedience.

Day 190

IN THE SECRET PLACE

He that dwelleth in the secret place of the most high God is at a major advantage. There are things that happen in the secret place that adds value to the relationship that you have with Christ. It is the place where your relationship is consummated with him. It is the place where he shares secret nuggets with you, about you, as an individual, and he brings clarity to corporate things as well. This is also the place where he changes your wineskin so that you are not stuck trying to put new wine in old wineskin and create a spiritual catastrophe. The secret place....dwell there, abide there, stay there, and grow there.

IF THEY CAN'T CONNECT WITH YOU,
THEY WILL KILL YOU!

Isn't it interesting how the people who are closest to you will crucify you when they feel that they can no longer connect to you? I remember when my first book came out and I was on tour. Life went completely bonkers for me. Naturally, I had to hire help because my life felt like it was spiraling out of control. Immediately when people found themselves talking to my personal assistant because I was busy, they began the crucifixion of my character. They thought that I had become "Hollywood" in my mentality. Very few of them took the time to ask me what was going on, and why I had a personal assistant. They just immediately drew their own incorrect conclusions. This same kind of activity happens when you begin to grow in Christ. They say you are acting funny; they call you names like "Holy Roller" and the like. Yes, it hurts, but stay focused it's the first level of Christian growth when you outgrow the former things and people of life.

Day 192

THE REAL ME

Many times we are taught, either explicitly or implicitly, to mask our issues or sweep them under the rug rather than to deal with them. Our pain is minimized and our pressure is overlooked. This is what causes for many of us to self-medicate through other means, such as drugs and alcohol, and can also lead to depression and other mental ailments that are very real, but also all a manifestation of something bigger and deeper. So before it gets to that level, let's act proactively and really deal with the issues of life as they come, and seek help when needed. It could literally mean life or death to you both spiritually, mentally and emotionally.

Day 193

NOT AN EQUAL OPPOSITE

It is interesting how when we were in the world, we were what I call, "Chief Sinners." We were the life of the party, on time if not early for an event, frequent flyer to the club scene and the like. We were just able to roll with the best of them on every hand. That is one opposite. Then when we come to Christ, we lay low in our worship experiences, late for the one Sunday morning worship that we do attend, only come to church for Sunday worship but never seeking to learn more of him in Sunday School or Bible Study. This is the other opposite. When we choose to cheat God of all the effort that we gave to the devil, I call this, "not an equal opposite." There should be more effort in getting acclimated to the life of holiness as there was in getting to know the life that we lived with the enemy. We have no choice; we have some making up to do.

Day 194

SPIRITUAL SOCIAL SECURITY

The Bible tells us not forsake the assembly of ourselves with other saints. Have you ever wondered why? I have. The reason why is because there is spiritual security in the socialization of the saints. When we come together, we can network one with the other and be helpers one to another. We can share our strengths and struggles with each other and if there is an issue that we have already overcome, then we can share how we overcame it. This is where the spiritual social security comes in. The caring is in the sharing. The sharing is in the building. The building is for the edification of the relationship. We must be helpers one to another so that we all know that we are not alone.

Day 195

WHEN LAZARUS CAME FORTH

We should be excited whenever we hear the story of how Lazarus came forth. This occurrence is a direct reflection of God's manifestation in our lives. This is a testament of how God can take a dead thing to us and resurrect it to life and the fullness thereof. He can bring your marriage back to life. He can bring your health back to life. He can bring your sanity back to life. He can bring your finances back to life. He can do it! The question is, "Will you pursuit him as fervently as the family of Lazarus did?" "Will you show the real and raw emotions that they did when they were displeased with his timing?" God already knows how you feel, so there is no need to hide or harbor emotions and feelings when it comes to him. Be honest with him and watch him call your miracle to come forth.

Day 196

THE MOBILITY OF THE ENEMY

Why do we stand still when the enemy is mobile? Peter tells us that our adversary, the devil, like a roaring lion, walketh about seeking whom he may devour. He goes on to say that, "he who stands fast "in the faith" will experience the greatness of the God of all Grace. I think that many of us misinterpret the "stand" to be a literal term and that is not what it means. The way to fight the enemy is not in the standing, but in the falling on your face, and seeking the face of God. Don't stand still while the enemy is moving and dancing on the top of your head. Move in your worship, move in your praise, and watch God move in your circumstance and your situation.

Day 197

4 C's of Accountability

Romans 8:28
*²⁸ And we know that all things work together for good to them that love God,
to them who are the called according to his purpose.*

Accountability is the one thing that we all need, but we often hate. The great thing about God is that he always forewarns us before destruction comes but even more so he gives us strategies and tactics to keep us from falling prey at the hands of the enemy. First thing he does is cautions us of the peril that is to come. Then he reminds us that we were called for such a time as this. Because we were called, there is a charge that is associated with that call. The hard part is that there is a consequence associated with every decision that we make in reference to all of these C's of accountability.

- Caution
- Call-to summon by or if by divine command
- Charge-a duty or responsibility laid upon or entrusted to one
- Consequence-an act or instance of following something as an effect, result or outcome

MY MATURITY EXEMPLIFIED

I remember when I became a teenager; I thought that I had arrived. I felt as though I knew everything and that the world was a puzzle to everyone else but me. I know that this is a phase that we all go through, but something happened to me when my mother died, less than 30 days after I turned 18. Luckily, I was already living on my own with my daughter, but I remember crying out to God and telling him I didn't really know how to be grown and I heard him ever so clearly. "Just be it!" Now, I was more confused than ever before because I didn't know what "it" was. Finally, he revealed that there is a difference in being grown and being mature. I had always been mature for my age, even though I wasn't grown. He told me that mature saints find the glory while they're in the storm, and baby saints find the glory after the fact. Mature individuals are proactive, and babies are reactive. Now that I got that part, the "it" was easier to understand. "It" was maturity. Don't talk about "it", just be "it." Exemplify your maturity in all your ways, and it will take you much further than hollering about how grown you are.

I GOT GRACE FOR THIS

Just as we have to develop our faith, we also have to develop our grace. Grace comes when we face adversity and we have to find strength to carry on. Grace and unmerited favor are gifts that are given to us, but when I say we develop our grace, I mean that we have to learn not to take it for granted. We learn that just because we have grace anew each morning, it does not mean that we have to use it up by indulging in the same issues and sins of our former days. The more interesting thing about grace is that God gives us a measure of grace to endure certain trials and tribulations. That is why we all handle situations differently. It's another reason why the scripture reads, "the God of all grace." So when you go through a storm, remember that you were favored that opportunity because God knows that you have the ability to endure it with grace and in grace.

FROM INTELLECT TO INFORMATION

As a highly intellectual individual, I had to learn the difference between intellect and information and when to use what. See intellect is from man, but the information that really matters is the revelation that comes from God. Speaking what God has told me about me and what I need to do based on what he says, far supersedes any book knowledge that I may have. I had to come to the realization that there is a time and a place for each of these occurrences. Discern the timing to use each in your life and get a revelation of how, and when, to operate in them.

Day 201

I CAN'T STOP IT AND YOU CAN'T EITHER

When you are anointed to do a thing for Christ, it is interesting how people want you to turn it off and on for their convenience. If only it were that easy. This is part of the reason why I am so skeptical about the people that I hang around, because when they discover your gift and/or talent, they have a tendency to try to exploit it for their own good. I remember trying to be in relationships with people, and as soon as they realized that I had the gift of prophesy, they would take me around their friends and as soon as we left the gathering they would ask questions like, "What did you see?" "Tell me about so and so?" This was my sign to quickly exit stage left. I then learned that you have to teach people how to be around you when you are gifted. It goes back to teaching people how to treat you, and how to respect the boundaries that you create for them according to your level of comfort and ability.

THE SAFETY OF MY HEART

In every relationship, we always seek for a safe place for our hearts. A place where we are safe to be transparent. A place where we are able to be who we are authentically called to be. A place where we can exhale and consider ourselves able to be safe and sound. A place where our hearts can be content, and our minds at ease. Well, my dear friends, I am glad to tell you that the only place that this experience can exist is in Christ. Christ is the only place where your heart is safe. God knows the intricacies of your heart and your being. He created your heart, so surely he knows how to care for it and what it takes to make it beat. Give your heart to him and know that it is safe there.

WHERE IS YOUR EDEN?

Eden is a place of a spiritual a spiritual dichotomy. It was a place where there is purity and everything was provided, but it was also a place where deception took place and reality was exposed. For this devotional, we are going to look at the latter. The question of the day is, "Where is your Eden?" The place where you became delusional and lost your way. The place where you made the decision that changed the whole element of your life. The place where you found yourself straying from God and doing the direct opposite of what he told you to do. The interesting thing is that in that place, purity was lost, but can also be found. Adam and Eve were as pure as pure could get. They had everything that they needed and wanted literally at their fingertips, but because of the deception of the enemy and their disobedience, purity was taken away from them and reality set in. After doing the direct opposite of what God told them to do, they were forgiven, sure enough, but the consequences still remained. Again, I ask where is your Eden?

WHAT ABOUT ME?

How many times in our lives have we suffered from the state I like to call, "What about me syndrome." This is where and when you become dissolutioned with all of the hats that you wear; parent, sister, brother, son, daughter, student, employee, professional, leadership etc. It is the days when you become overwhelmed by the hats and you want to scream and say, "What about me?" Those days when you just want to scream and holler, and you are being pulled in a million different directions and it seems you don't have enough hands and no one is trying to lend a hand to ensure that all needs are met. These are what I call, "What about me days." These are the days you have to lean on the strength of God to get through, and trust me, we all have them, and it's only by the grace of God that we get through them. Nevertheless, in the midst of it all remember that you are not alone.

Day 205

DON'T FAKE WHAT YOU CAN FIX

I remember as a kid, my brother and I, or at least my brother, was an extreme wrestling fan. I hated wrestling because every time after the show went off, he would practice all the wrestling moves on me. There were numerous times he would break things and I would try to be the handy girl and fix it so mom wouldn't notice it. Now as a parent myself, I have seen my children do the same things. Now in our character, there are flaws that we know are wounded and in error, but yet we still try to fake it and put on the façade that we are ok. The truth of the matter is that we are not ok and everything is not fine and we are in such turbulence at times that we don't know if we are going or coming. The question is, "Why fake it when you know that you can fix it?" Why be strong when in reality you are really weak? Do you feel as though it makes you less of a person? Does it make you appear weak? The truth of the matter is that you are weak, and that is the state of being that God can capitalize on because he said, "Where you are weak, there I am strong." So don't fake what you can fix. Tell the truth about the matter and allow the Lord to mend you right where you hurt.

IT'S TIME TO GROW UP!

GROW UP! Stop letting the enemy get the best of you. GROW UP! You can still make your dreams come true. GROW UP! See God for who he truly is. GROW UP! Quit crying over things that cannot be changed, find the things that can be changed and change them. Everyone has a story, everyone has a past. No one really came up with a silver spoon in their mouths and if they did, trust me that they paid for it in one way or another. So get a grip, GROW UP, and move on with life!

I'M NOT AN AFTERTHOUGHT

I am so glad that God didn't think of me after he created the earth. I am glad that he didn't think of me after he was worn out and tired. I am so glad that he didn't think of me and use leftover materials to create me. With all of this greatness in mind, my question is, "Why do we make ourselves afterthoughts?" It is important that we put ourselves first because we have to first be filled before we can be of any assistance to anyone else. See when the Bible talks about our cups overflowing, you are the cup, you must first be filled before you can give the overflow to others. Stop making yourself an afterthought because God thought of you first and you should do the same.

WHEN CRIPPLED MEETS HANDICAPPED

When we seek to be in a relationship, we want to make sure that we are first whole in and of ourselves. There are a number of reasons why this has to occur in this order. The first reason is because when we are in pursuit of our mate, we often times attract what we are. If you are incomplete and not whole, you are likely to attract the same. The worst thing that can happen is crippled meets handicapped and then reproduce something disabled. In this scenario, there is no function in the relationship as a whole. Even more detrimental is that the family will begin to perceive dysfunction as functional. This creates a cycle that will likely be duplicated for generations to come. This is where the root of generational curses begin. The best way to war against this effort is to prevent it by starting off as a whole.

THE ULTIMATE HEALER

The great thing about God is that not only is he a healer, but he is the ultimate healer. What is the difference? I am glad that you asked! See a healer waits until you are sick to prescribe what you need to treat your infirmity. The Ultimate healer is the one and only that can heal you before the sickness even manifests. Not only that, but he is able to heal you, not only of the superficial, but take that healing all the way to the root of the problem. There is never a pill to take, there is no cost to the care, you don't have a premium, and it's yours simply for the asking. Take your issues to him today and receive the manifestation of your healing.

YES I GOT _____, BUT DID YOU NOTICE I DIDN'T DIE?

We all go through adversity, and there are times when adverse reactions happen to us in the midst of the storm. Immaturity would have us to cry about the things that happened to us during that time. I call it the time that we practice and rehearse reciting the pain, which is pointless. Maturity is able to recite the things you lost, but put a positive twist on the end stating the most important thing that happened. Yes, I got hurt, but did you notice I didn't die? Yes, I got heartbroken, but did you notice I didn't die? Yes, I got betrayed, but did you notice I didn't die? Yes, I got lied on, but did you notice I didn't die? YOU DIDN'T DIE, SO MOVE ON!

LAUNCH IN THE DEEP, JUST DON'T DROWN

When God gives us a promise, we have to ensure that we have the balance that is needed to receive the promise. We have to make sure that we heed to ALL of the instructions, before we leap. Oftentimes, when we receive a promise, we react in different ways. We either don't move due to fear, or we talk ourselves out of it, or even worst we tip toe instead of running when he says so. Now is the time that we should be ready to reap the harvest of what we have sown and been believing God for. Stop being scared, stop allowing the enemy to speak to you and talk you out of your blessing. Stop procrastinating! Launch into the deep, but be careful that you don't drown. This means take your progress in stride and don't sprint at the starting line and crawl to the finish line. Take it all in stride. One day at a time, one step at a time. I am talking to you as I am talking to myself. As an author, I am so passionate about writing that when I released my first book, I made a goal of putting out one book every year for the rest of my life. Well, life happened and after 2013 I didn't put a book out for a while. Well when I rededicated myself to my craft, I decided to keep my promise to myself and write 5 books in one year which is unheard of. Unheard of or not, I was committed to doing it. Now I understood that there was no way I could write all five at once so I took it in stride and completed one book at a time. This devotional was a project that I had been working on since 2013 but just never finished, and because I knew that it would take the longest. I completed this one first and then swiftly moved on to the next one. This is a prime example of what I mean when I say, "Launch into the deep, but just don't drown."

Day 212

I FORCED MYSELF IN, BUT CRIED MYSELF OUT

We have all found ourselves in a position that we felt, or better yet, that we knew we had no business being in. Places that we know God didn't ordain for us to go, but yet we went in anyway. We have been with people that we knew were not good for us, yet we remain in the relationship. These are the places that we force ourselves into and find ourselves having to cry ourselves out. The silver lining in all of this is that you should walk away from the experience with a greater appreciation for obedience. It also lessens the likelihood that you will go back to this place of disobedience because you will see the difficulty of getting out of situations that you place yourselves in. We all have been in this place before, and there is nothing that says we won't ever go back into this place, but when you cry yourself out, you are less likely to enter into this place again.

DROP IT

Gone are the days that we sit around eating sorrow sandwiches crying about how we got over! Gone are the days that we sit around and rehearse the pain that we were graced to make it through. Gone are the days that we compare our pains and heartaches with others and race to the greater victim seat. Now are the days that we drop it! I know you have been hurt, but now is the time to drop it! I know you have been through pain, but now is the time to drop it! I know you have been misled, but now is the time to drop it! Now understand that dropping it doesn't mean that you forget it, it just means that it's time for healing. Think of it this way, your past is a healed wound, but every time that you talk about it, be it completely healed or not, you are ripping that wound wide open. Not a clean cut, but a jagged rip. You also are adding infection to it when people show you affection and pet you up in your pain. The sad part is that it's not even their fault, but the fact that you haven't matured to your place of healing is evident. So now is the time to grow up, and drop it!

Day 214

NO DEVIATION, NO DISTRACTION, JUST DIRECTION

When we receive a directive from the Lord, it is not our duty to question it, but it is a place to stay focused. Focus on the directive. Put your eye on the prize and don't take it off. There is nothing to consult with people about because after all it is your directive and not theirs. People will try to show you the quickest deviation out of your promise; they will distract your praise, and direct you away from what it is that God told you to do. Two lessons to take from this; be careful who you share your directives with and only do it God's way, not the way of man. His way may be the hard way, and it may seem like it's only going to take you longer, but I promise you if you stay focused you will be there in no time.

*Day 215*

THE CRITICAL NATURE OF CIRCUMCISION

When we hear the word circumcision, we automatically think of the procedure performed on most male children shortly after they are born. However, when we look in the Bible we see the responsibility that we have to circumcise our hearts. What does this mean? It means that there is a cutting away, a pruning so to speak, that must take place in order for your heart to flourish in the newness of Christ. If you try to pass up the circumcision, you will be more prone to infection in latter days, such as unforgiveness and the harboring of other negative feelings. So it is critical that you circumcise your heart and mind to be able to grow and mature in Christ.

SAVED AND IGNORANT

It is critical that we move past the stage and state of being saved. Many people feel as though it is enough to just be saved. This mindset makes no sense. Think of your dream possession. What if someone walked in and gave you your dream home and they even gave you the keys, but you never moved into it, would you still be able to enjoy it? What about your dream car? What if they gave you the car, but you didn't know how to drive. Would that motivate you to learn? So it should be in the body of Christ. When you receive Christ as your personal savior, you inherit keys to the kingdom and the fullness thereof, but if you never learn of your inheritance, you are forcing yourself to live beneath the privilege to which God gives you access. So take his yoke upon you and learn of him so that you won't be saved and ignorant living beneath the poverty line of the Kingdom.

STUDY TO SHUT UP

The Bible says, "Thy word have I hid in my heart so that I may not sin against thee (Psalms 119:11)." If you hide a thing do you holler from the mountain top its location? No! Exactly, when it is hidden it is a secret so to speak. So it is with the Kingdom. Our lives should be the testament of our relationship with the master. We have to be able to show people our witness instead of telling them our witness. Our witness is also held comparable to what we study. Stop running through the marketplace broadcasting how much you love Christ and just let your light so shine that people can see your good words and know who it is that you serve. Don't be so busy talking your head knowledge; let your heart knowledge show. Be still and know that I am God.

Day 218

From Theology to Therapy

One of the many points of therapy is to show you what you already know, and how to apply it to your everyday practices and keep it in the front of your mind. I am sorry to say, there are no hidden truths that are revealed to you in therapy, but it just gives you another way of looking at a matter. So it is with theology. Theology is nothing magical, it simply teaches you about the religious faith, practices and experiences. The spiritual therapy comes in the reconciling of what we have been taught through tradition and denomination, to what the word actually says about a matter. So as you see the process goes from theology to therapy which is the foundation of the relationship that you establish between you and God alone.

I Don't Need Healing,
I Need to be Challenged

It is so interesting, but also challenging, being a seasoned veteran for the Kingdom. I encounter all kinds of issues, especially when people see that I have my PhD in Christian Education. Oftentimes, there are even those who are intimidated until they get to know me and realize that I am not one of those that think that they know everything. I love to learn and so I enjoy hearing other people's perspective about scripture. It doesn't mean that I eat from every table, at which I sit, but I do love to be challenged in my thinking and I have always been that way. I urge all leaders to think about the manners in which you teach forums such as Bible study and Sunday school, and realize that there are not just babies but there are seasoned saints as well. As a seasoned saint, please don't forget us and if we ask a challenging question, don't pray us away or say we need healing, we just want to be challenged in our learning too.

CONSIDER IT FIRST!

How many times have we thoroughly thought through a thing before acting on it? Especially, when it comes to repeating an act like being in a less than healthy relationship. No worries, we all have fallen prey to this tactic of the enemy a time or two. When I did it, not only in personal relationships, but also business relationships, I would always give them the benefit of the doubt only to find myself hurt yet again. Since then, I have learned not to live my life in reverse anymore. My new motto is, "consider it first!" Consider everything, not just the positives, but also remember why the relationship ended in the beginning. Remember the pain and the hurt that you felt the last time you encountered this person and situation, and then pray on it and make the decision then. Oftentimes, we remember one side because the other side is too painful to remember, but I urge you that the next time that you think of going reverse consider it all first.

DON'T SWITCH ON ME NOW!

How many times have we all made decisions that turned out less than favorable. Times when we have cried about that thing, prayed about that thing and even consulted with friends, which is probably the worst thing to do, but we did it. Then when that situation turns out less than favorable or just flat out wrong all odds are against you, then it seems that everyone turns their back on you. This is one of the most painful experiences of abandonment that one can experience, but yet we all go through it. This is what I call the "switcheroo." The place where the very friend that you consulted about the matter and they give you their advice, whether you took it or not, and things turn out worst and then they begin to sing their, "I told you so" song. The great thing about this place is that it is a place where you will surely discover who your friends are. This is the place where God definitely does the separating of the tares from the wheat. Let him separate them and as you go through the painful experience of the separation from those tares, just trust God because he will never switch on you. He is the same yesterday, today and forevermore.

WHO IS IN YOUR ARMY?

I remember when I was a little girl; we would sing this song that speaks of us being in the army of the Lord. I used to get so tired of hearing this song and of course those are the songs that we all remember. As a child, I was raised by military parents that took us all over the world. When my father was in the military, I learned at an early age how to embrace the differences in cultures and geographic locations. From that experience, I was trained to, as an adult, to respect different perspectives and opinions. More than that, it also taught me how to inspect my comradery of friends and associates and group them accordingly. It taught me to keep an eye on the army that I am a part of and which ones to keep at bay, while there are others that I can authentically trust. Why am I telling you this? Good question! I am telling you because you need to ensure that you evaluate your army from time to time to ensure that you are receiving what you need, but more so, that you are able to give them what they need without overexerting yourself. Check your circle and make sure that it is a healthy fit for all involved.

EACH ONE, REACH ONE OR MORE

What would happen in our local churches if every Sunday each person brought a new person to church? This is evangelism at its finest. Yes, this is a great theory and methodology, but why doesn't it happen? Could it be that we are ashamed of our worship centers? Could it be that we don't want to share our worship experience with others because it is sacred to us and we are selfish in our experiences? Could it be that the life that we live is not inviting to others that are not in Christ? There are, and could be, so many reasons why this doesn't happen, but whatever the reason, you will grow to regret it in the days to come. Do you know that there is a jewel that goes into your crown in the kingdom for every soul that you bring to Christ? If that don't get you going, I don't know what will. Let's get busy, share our faith, and let our worship be a witness to those around us so that God can get the glory.

I Won't Lay in Your Sewer

The sad thing about many people in our world today is that they really do have the crab in the bucket mentality. For the few of you who may have never heard of this analogy, it is where when a crab tries to get out of the bucket, the others pull it back down to keep them inside the bucket with them. The way that this compares to humans is that when we try to come out of the bondage or situations and circumstances that we are familiar with, there are those who will tell us all the reasons why we shouldn't change, why we should stay where they are, how what we are trying to do is not going to work. When they come to you with this, be sure to tell them that you will not partake in their stinking thinking and that you refuse to lie in their sewer of negative thinking.

PULPIT PROSTITUTION

One would never think that there is a prostitution ring in the body of Christ, but indeed it happens all of the time. Pulpit prostitution is where a leader elevates members, or uses the members for their own selfish gain. What are those selfish gains? Glad you asked! They elevate them or assign them to responsibilities to keep them from leaving, to reward them for their tithes and offerings that are above the norm, to make them become more vested to the ministry, or even to help to grow their own ministry. I myself have been prostituted in my experiences and it was for all of the reasons above which is why I can speak on it with such conviction. This madness made me upset, bitter, and literally made me walk away from the church for a season. Woe to the leaders who do this because it literally can make one stumble and fall. So beware, be honest, when you are called to elevation in God, it should come as a confirmation to you, and not an affirmation of you. This thinking is the simplest way to separate the motive of the leader for your elevation.

Day 226

Sour Lemons to Sweet Lemonade

As children, many of us were told that when life gives you lemons, to just make lemonade. We have all had some bitter lemonade that was a little less than desirable to the taste. This fact has caused me to be more specific in my verbiage and I have purposed in my head and heart to turn my entire situation around. Yes, that thing happened to me, but it does not define who I am, or how I am, it was an occurrence. Yes, I even did that thing more than once, but guess what; it still doesn't change the great potential that God has invested in me. I purposed in my heart to make the soul choice that the sour lemons I have been given in life, that I will add the sweetness of the word of God to it, and the chill of experience, and make some great tasty lemonade. Will you make that same choice? I hope so, because life is too short to look bitter.

INSANITY NO MORE!

Tell yourself and all of the imps assigned to you that I am going through a transition called, "Insanity No More!" No longer will I focus on the negative that has happened to me! No longer will I allow the enemy to play with my mind and emotions and make me feel as though I deserve anything less than God's best for my life! I can't believe I gave anyone that much power over my life. I now know my worth! I now know that I really can do all things through Christ who strengthens me! I understand that I am the head and not the tail, the lender and not the borrower! I have the power to win over every satanic attack that the enemy throws my way! I am a king's kid! I am royalty! So stop the insanity devil, I know who I am!

CORPORATE COMMUNICATION, INDIVIDUAL RELATION

The Bible tells us not to forsake the assembling of ourselves with the saints, however many of us feel as though we can make it without assembling. We ask questions like, "Why do I need to go to church? I am the church! I can talk to God at home!" While this is all true, you still need to assemble with the saints because of the simple fact that #1 it is a commandment, but more than that we draw strength from one another. See corporate worship is all about communicating with not only God, but also the saints as well! It is all about the corporate nature of Christ. We get strength in knowing that we are not alone in the issues that we go through. We see that the same God that brought them out can bring us out as well. When we are alone we are more apt to be attacked by the lying demon that tells us that we are alone and that no one cares about neither us nor what we go through. This is why the enemy likes to keep us isolated because we are more apt to be defeated and fall in to residual side effects such as depression and suicide and the likes that will keep us bound and away from our God given talent, call, gift and destiny.

DICTATION OF MY DESTINY?

Isn't it crazy to think that there are actually people out there who feel as though we can't reach our appointed place in God without them? They feel that because they are not a part of your life that you will not, shall not, and cannot make it. We all know that this is a lie from the pits of hell, but how many of us have fell into the trap of this thinking. I remember the first solo cd that I put out, I felt like I could not complete the rest of the cd without the person who did the single with me. I felt like he held the keys to the kingdom of my musical life. After all, he was the one who challenged me to write my first song by myself. He was the one who developed me as an artist. I gave so much credit to him as a person, that it only made sense for God to remove him because he was gladly taking the credit that only belonged to God. Listen my friends, no one can dictate your destiny but God, and your destiny was established before you were even created. If you fail to keep this fact in the forefront of your mind as you pursuit your various endeavors in life, he will continue to remove the people from your life who you feel have to be there in order to be successful because remember he told us that he is a jealous God and no one can and will be put before him.

AROUND THE FIRE, BUT STILL COLD!

Have you ever been camping and started a campfire and yet you were still effected by the cold of night? Have you sat there and shivered as the night air blew across your skin. You were close to the fire, but you were still cold. How could this be? Cannot fire overtake the bitterness of the cold? Cannot the energy and exertion that you use when you shiver be enough to at least get you to some other level of comfort? This same truth holds true in Christendom. The ultimate fire is the Holy Ghost that is used and indwells in all of us in some manner or another. How can we attend church every Sunday and function in any magnitude in the church and still be cold spiritually? How can we take communion, do praise and worship, and some even preach the word and still fall into the category of the Christian that God will spew out of his mouth? The answer is clear; we refuse to yield our will to his and to make his will ours. We get close enough to say that we were in attendance, but not close enough that the fire consumes us and changes us from day to day. This is a dangerous place to be because if judgment comes before you get it right, you will be the one who is left behind. So jump in the fire and be ye consumed before it's too late.

Day 231

YOU CANNOT CAST OUT OF THE SANCTUARY WHAT IS IN YOUR HEART!

There is a great book on the market called "Pigs in the Parlor" that deals with warfare. Whenever I prepare to do a warfare conference, I always assign new staff to read it so that they can see the detriment of the efforts that we are about to embark upon. In my warfare conferences and workshops, I always tell the people of the ways in which warfare can be achieved and it starts not with the individuals who come for deliverance, but for the person that God is using to perform the deliverance service. Many people find this fact interesting because they think that it is all about oiling people down and praying, and some even think that it is about the shouting and screaming, but here is the naked truth! It starts with you! It starts with what is in your heart. How can one pray unforgiveness out of someone else when they have it in their hearts? What really happens is that those spirits, the one in you and the one in them reproduce like spirits in others. You cannot pray fornication off of people when you participate in the same act. This is the most hypocritical act of the believers and most leaders. When I went through my season of homosexuality, I dared not pray over anyone who was wrestling with that spirit until I knew that I was free and clean from it, otherwise we just affirmed what was in both of our hearts and made it almost virtually impossible to break free from it. So as you begin to lay hands and pray for others examine yourself first to make sure that you are good in that area, if you're not, it does not take away from you to pass the baton to someone else who is not wrestling with the same issue. Let wisdom have her perfect work.

DON'T BE WHERE YOU DON'T FIT!

When you give your life to Christ, there are certain sectors that you just don't fit into, but there are also relationships that you are still a part of that you don't feel the need to end because it seems harmless. Though it may be true that the relationships are harmless, you have to be careful that those relationships don't pull you back into places that you have been delivered from. When we are delivered from things that our associates are still in bondage with, it makes it more difficult for us to stay free, especially when we are new to Christendom and we enter into the churches that tell us all of the "no" and none of the options that there are. This is one of the ways we wind up in places that we don't belong. There is always that period in your walk where you don't fit in with the world because you gave your life to Christ, and not even so much that you changed, but they perceive a change and they are uncomfortable with it. Then there is the issue that you don't fit in with the church either, you are not quite enough to run with them. To them, you still dress like the world, your language may not be totally holy, and God forbid you partake in a sin. This is the point where many Christians go into isolation and a spirit of depression and loneliness forms. Those spirits will tell you all the reasons why you should remain in the clubs or doing all manners of things that are contrary to the will of God. Guard yourself with his word, find you a church that is not about the "no" but is all about taking and replacing so that you don't fall into the bland nature of the traditional Christian. You can do this....just keep going!

463

ATTENDANCE IS NOT....

Attendance is not salvation,

Just because you go to church, does not guarantee you a seat in the kingdom.

Attendance is not commitment,

Just because you attend on Christmas, Mother's Day and Easter doesn't make you a member.

Attendance is not productivity,

Just because you go, does not mean that you apply rules and principles to your life to produce fruit.

Attendance is not just being present,

Being present is great, but until you accept the present that Christ is trying to give, it is for naught!

Examine your reason, rationale and motive as to why you do the things you do. Why do you attend what you attend? What are you doing there? Are you growing or are you just present? Are you changing or just remaining? Are you able to apply the principles and skills to your life? If your answers are less than favorable, it may be time to make a change.

Day 234

SAVED TO SERVE

When we accept Christ as our personal Savior, it is about the security of salvation, but is more about the service that you are called to render after the fact. Many people feel as though there is nothing to do if you are not in the forefront singing, dancing, preaching and other manners of leadership, but just remember that you were called to serve in any capacity. I for one, though I am a preacher, praise and worship leader, teacher and many other things, I actually like the other noble side that involves being in the background such as cleaning the church, serving on home committees and the like. Believe it or not, those are the servant positions that bring about no pressure nor nerves. So as you go through life, just remember that you are called to serve, and not just to salvation.

YOU CAN'T REBUKE WHAT YOU CAN'T RESIST

One of the most common warfare errors is when we try to rebuke a thing that we are not ready to release. You can rebuke with your words all you want, but until you are prepared to release that thing for good, it will remain in your presence until the end of time. I remember years ago a friend of mine wrote a play, and in the play the teen girl was running through the aisle screaming, "Satan, I rebuke you!" While she was doing that, Satan was running right next to her mocking her and repeating everything that she said. This was a play, but it is the brutal reality of what really happens when we try to rebuke a thing that we choose to hold on to. So give it up and let it go!

GREAT LEADERS CONSIDER GOD'S HEART

There are levels of leaders. There are leaders, then there are good ones and finally there are great ones. Regular leaders are the one who are able to influence the people and get them to do what they want done. They have no real vison or purpose, but they do have an agenda, be it hidden or exposed. Good ones are the ones that consider the hearts of the people because the people walk away with a sense that their needs have been met, but there is no real growth, it's just an itch that has been scratched, but there is no real expectation for elevation. Finally, there are great leaders who are the ones who consider God's heart in all of their affairs. They find a way to reconcile what I call the triad of great leader. They meet the needs and expectations of God first and foremost, the needs of the people secondly and then they allow their needs to be met and supplied in abundance by virtue of their obedience. Great leaders understand that there is no one way to do a thing outside of God's way. They understand that if they acknowledge God in all of their ways that he will supply all of their needs to include the people that they need to help the vison to go forth and then the people will ensure that the household of faith is supplied for as well. This is the divine order of provision for a leader that considers God's heart.

Day 237

LIFE IS A FISHBOWL

(PEOPLE ARE WATCHING FROM EVERY ANGLE)

Sometimes I marvel at the mediums that God uses to give me a revelatory word. One day I was in PetSmart with my grandson who loves animals. He was only a year old at the time. We were looking at the little fish in the fishbowl. He was so excited he kept screaming, "Ohhh, Grammy Look!!!" Keep in mind that I was already looking at the same fish however, I didn't see it from his view as he was much smaller and looking at it from his standpoint, he saw something different and he wasn't satisfied until I bent down to look at it from his perspective. That's when the word came to me that life is a fishbowl and you are just the fish. People are watching you from every angle and what they see from their perspective and experience with you is what they believe you to be. God sees you from the North, the heavenlies, and he knows you to be one way. Family members and friends see you from the west and believe that they know you best. Enemies see you from the east and become a beast in your life to try to distract and bother you to keep you from reaching your God given destiny. But it's the people whose life you have impacted in one way or another that see you from the south. They don't know and really don't care about your story, you are just simply someone who has impacted their life and they look up to you. As you go about your day, remember that there are people looking from every angle and they all have different perspectives and agendas for you so, in all of your being, be authentic.

FROM INSANITY TO INTEGRITY

I remember when I was first exposed to dating; I had no clue what I was doing. I thought that it was all about getting as many numbers as you could and meeting as many people as you could. Yes, in your mind you had an agenda of what you wanted, but the point of the race was to meet as many and then make the eliminations accordingly if they didn't line up with my expectations of a perfect mate. Do they even exist? Nevertheless, this insanity of thinking went on for much too long. Finally, I woke up and realized that the people who I was dealing with hard feelings too and the world didn't revolve around me and my eliminations without explanation. This is when I went from insanity to integrity. Integrity came when I would take my time to get to know one person at a time and would explore that person from the inside out. The insanity of trying to keep up with their facts, which was a lot of pressure, was alleviated when I made this decision. Maybe it's not dating that is your insanity. Perhaps it's just simply putting too many things on your plate at once and doing a lot of things, but not doing anything well. Slow down and deal with one thing at a time. Only you know what that "thing" is. Explore it, and do it well, then move on to the next task.

MY SECRET STORM

How many storms have we all gone through where we felt as though we couldn't and wouldn't tell anyone what was going on. We held that storm dear to our hearts for fear of ridicule and shame and of course judgement. There are all types of storms that we choose to keep a secret so we paste on the phony smiles on our faces, and we put on our hallelujah hats and we dance all over the storm only to return to it in our own private time. This is where the spiritual and emotional roller coaster comes in, and it only opens the door for other issues to manifest and in turn you keep those a secret as well and before you know it, you are living a lie and in a secret world of deceit. From the place, no good thing can be birthed, but more and more issues. The first thing to understand is that you cannot hide anything from God, and ultimately he is the one to share it with and more importantly he is the only one that can do something about it. Just be honest and allow him into your secret storm and watch him work it out.

Day 240

I DARE YOU TO TRY!

We are not healed in our hearing of the word, but the doing therein. How many times has God given you a task to do but yet you resist it out of fear or even worst out of failure? How many times do you see a need in your church, your home, and/or your community, but you refuse to take on the task because it has never been done. Perhaps there is a need that someone is meeting, and they appear to be successful in it, but God shows you a greater way, a more effective way to make a greater impact, and yet for whatever reason you choose to stand still and watch the opportunity bypass you and your household. Whatever the situation is, I dare you to try it. I dare you to seek to live above your current level. I dare you to try your own business! I dare you to compete with the common mentality of your surroundings. I dare you to step out and be greater than the greatest you have ever seen.

Day 241

THE SEARCH ENGINE OF THE HOLY GHOST

Some people call it intuition, some people call it "something", but the wise and mature know it to be the Holy Ghost. How many times were you about to jump into a thing and "something" told you not to do it? Have you ever walked into your house, as a parent, and just felt like something wasn't right? These are all reactive scenarios, but the great thing about the Holy Ghost is that he is available to be used proactively as well. Whenever you are seeking to make a decision or to embark upon a new venture in your life, I dare you to reach out to the Holy Ghost and allow him to lead you into all truths. When you use the search engine of the Holy Ghost, he will protect you from all hurt, harm or danger. When you use the search engine of the Holy Ghost, it will keep you from getting your heartbroken because he will reveal the person to you to include their motives and intentions towards you. When you use the search engine of the Holy Ghost, he will keep you in perfect peace. This only happens when you use the search engine of the Holy Ghost.

I GAVE UP THAT FOR THIS?

Why is the failure rate of a convert being successfully saved, committed and converted so high? I think that an average of about six months as the going rate for a new convert to remain on fire for God is quite a giving number. When we as leaders seek out the reason and rationale for this number, I think that it is quite clear that we fail to give them alternatives for their former acts of fun. When people give their life to Christ it is for a number of reasons. One is just sheer desperation for something different. Another is that they just finished a service that was emotionally charged and they were guided by their emotions. Whatever the reason is that they came, we have to remember the days of our worldly state when there was always something to do, there were no limitations on what we could do, and the emotional charge that came with it all was consistent. The truth of the matter is that when people give their lives to Christ and they join the local church, they are told of all of the things that they CANNOT do and they are encouraged to give those things up with no alternative methodology for entertainment. Who would give a night on the town for a night to sit inside a church with a book in hand that they don't understand in a building with no color or charge? Who would give up their friends and rush to a line where they are at the end because their clothes don't align with the norm? We as Christians are leading people astray because they are left thinking, "I gave up that for this? The solution is clear make living right fun and exciting, fun doesn't have to be sinful and they need to know that, so give them options and make it clear that the best fun on earth keeps heaven in the vision clear.

Day 243

DON'T FAKE IT

What is the point of faking a thing? How long can one actually continue on the path of deceit before their true colors come out? It is not a matter of will it happen but when it will happen, that your true identity is on display for all to see. I heard it said once before that when one is dating someone new, for the first 90 days one is dating a representative of who that person is. If one can endure the first 90 days then the likelihood of entering into a true courtship is greater than just jumping into something that is not true or authentic. This truth comes and applies for both the women and the men. I always giggle when I meet people and they say yes, I am the one who you have been waiting and praying for, but yet upon our encounter, I can tell them ten reasons why I know that they are not the one. The point is, be authentic and true from day one and don't let your representative speak for you. The world will appreciate the authenticity of who you are.

Day 244

AS THY DAYS ARE SO SHALL THY STRENGTH BE!

We often encounter scriptures of a promise from God, and we always read it as though it is going to come to pass in days to come, but what about the present. This scripture reference that we are talking about today comes from a place of the present, but you have to see it in that manner. It says that your strength will be as long as your days. This is encouraging on every hand because if you just take a minute to reflect on the things that you have been through. Think of the absolute worst thing that you went through, that one thing that you never thought you would never make it through, but look at you know. Now you have to think to remember it. This is the encouraging piece of this scripture, because it teaches me that if God gave me an opportunity to experience this thing, he is going to give me the strength to get through it all, no matter how trying it is. Keep going and it will get better.

I HAVE TO FIND THE GLORY IN MY TRIBULATION

We have to go through our tribulations so that we can have the opportunity to find how God can get the glory out of this situation. Yes, I know it's hard to see it when you're in it, but just know that the devil had to get permission before he could even try you. There is nothing that the enemy can do to you unless God gives him the okay, and because God said that he would never give us more than we can bear, we have to trust that he knows that we have everything that we need to get through this thing before we even start it. So the next time you go through a storm, or even if you are in a storm right now, change your perspective of that thing and try to count the ways in which God can get the glory. After all it's all in the masterplan anyway.

WHAT WAS I THINKING?

Everyone has that encounter when you ask yourself, "What was I thinking?" What was I thinking when I agreed to this obligation? What was I thinking when I agreed to take this job? What was I thinking when I agreed to this relationship? What was I thinking when I made this business move? What was I thinking? This term often has a negative connotation to it, but let's flip the script and ask, "What was I thinking?" What was I thinking when I thought that God wouldn't make a way? What was I thinking when I have seen him, firsthand, handle bigger problems than this? What was I thinking when I doubted his presence in my storm. This is the thinking pattern that we should operate in on a daily basis and I promise it will encourage you to embrace other trials that may come your way because you will see him as the sovereign God that he is.

Day 247

HEALED ENOUGH TO KEEP GOING!

I am healed enough to keep going,
Though at times I want to quit,
I am healed enough to keep going,
Though I know that there are many opportunities that I have missed,
I am healed enough to keep going,
Though I said I couldn't, I wouldn't and I shouldn't.
I am healed enough to keep going,
Though the devil has tried to rip me to shreds and often succeeded because I fail to seek the face of the God head. Yes I am hurt, but I'm healed. Yes I bled, but I'm healed. Yes I cried, but I am healed. Yes I tried and failed, but guess what, I am still healed and it's in my going that I will be set free from the long term effects that could consume me. I will remember this trial just for the testimony. The details won't even matter because all that matters in the end if the fact that I am healed.

Day 248

I'VE GOT TO SLOW DOWN!

In this day of a microwave, internet, instantaneous delivery of promise, we, as a people, have become spoiled to the instant gratification of what it is that we need, want, and desire. Everything comes to us and we label it with a timeline and God forbid if things don't manifest in that time frame, the first thing we do is blame God. When was the last time you took a moment to just live in the moment? I mean put down cell phones in this generation of Facebook live and other forms of social media. When is the last time that you looked in the mirror and liked what you saw and DID NOT pull out the phone for that last selfie? Better yet, when was the last time that you spent quality time with family members, especially your children and banned all electronics for that sake of some quality family time. These are hard questions I am sure, but they are all an indication that we, as a society, must slow down and take a minute to live in the moment. Smell the flowers. Take a walk. Take a day without your cell phone. I promise you that you will survive, and you may even discover it to be rewarding to you. Try it!

THE ULTIMATE ITCH

When I gave my life to Christ at a young age, I had no idea the road that I was about to travel. I had no idea of the twists and turns that I would endure, nor the hardships that were to come. I was raised in a Baptist church, and back in those days no one talked about the Holy Ghost half as much as they do now. However, as I began to mature in Christ, thought I was still young in age, I knew that there had to be something more. I knew that there was a piece of me missing and I had no idea what it was. My mother was a church goer, but never really openly sought after revelation knowledge. My brother was so busy doing his own thing, and my step dad was not a part of the faith. Hungry for more, I began to have this spiritual yearning and longing, an itch if you will. Finally, I got it. I realized that I was remiss in utilizing the comforter that Christ left for us that would guide us in to all truth. When I received the baptism of the Holy Ghost with the evidence of speaking in tongues, my life was never the same again. I began to see all things differently! I began to understand scripture in a way that I was never able to before. As a child, I would sit on the pews and literally listen to the preacher preach, and God would speak to me in my terms so that I could understand what he was saying. Who wouldn't welcome a friend like that? You can't scratch the itch of the Holy Ghost. Nothing else compares to the companionship of the Holy Ghost.

DOG EAT DOG, AND GOD BE GOD

Many days, in this book, I have talked about perception and how we perceive things to be. Well today is no different, but I want to show you an eerie revealed word from the Lord using word play. How many times have you heard the term that this is a "dog eats dog" world where everyone is out for themselves, trying to "capitalize" on their own agendas in this world? Well if we just take a minute to flip the word Dog and see that it spells God, we will see that the change of perspective gives a whole new connotation to the saying. See with Dog eat Dog, it is all about capitalizing on self for selfish gain and no good thing can come from it. However, when we flip the word and the capitalization, it declares that no matter what I go through God is still God. This may be one of the greatest, most visible forms of revelation in this entire book. There is a change that is coming, but you have to be prepared for the change by changing your view and perception. So let the world be Dog eat Dog, I am sold on letting God be God!

RETIRING FROM SELF-CARE

When many people think of retirement, they think of it from a no longer working perspective. This book is all about spiritual revelation. The spiritual revelation of it all is the mere fact that retirement is much more than just no longer working, it takes on a whole new level of faith. The scenario is this; when you are working and you run across the need, there is the ability to work a few extra hours here and there to meet that need. However, once one retires, the ability to work a few extra hours here and there is no longer an option. This is where you get the revelation of retirement from self-care. There is a whole new level of faith that takes place when one is retired. To retire from self-care means to give up your will and yield to the will of the father and allow him to truly supply all of your needs. When you retire, you also give up control of your circumstance, and this puts it into perspective just for the sake of trusting the one and only. It's not easy, but it must be done, so go ahead and retire today, I guarantee you won't regret it.

THE STATE PATROL OF SANITY

As I was driving along one day I encountered a number of State Patrols on the side of the road. It wasn't a good day, might I add, because it was a day that I was in deep thought while driving and I wasn't paying attention to my speedometer, and of course I was one of the ones that they pulled over. Immediately I was taken out of prior thoughts to handle the matter at hand which was, "How do I get out of this without lying?" Immediately the Holy Ghost told me to just tell the truth. Though I know that you are not supposed to go against the Holy Ghost, nor ignore his orders, I just thought in my own head that will never work. When the officer got to my window I was preparing to give him my license and registration and all, but as I rolled down the window, he asked me, "What were you thinking about?" I was so thrown off kilter because in my natural mind, I was wondering how he knew that I was in thought. He went on to say, "I have been following you for some time and you never hit your brakes or anything and you ignored my lights." I looked at him and apologized for my actions. He told me to get out of the car and immediately, I began to fear of what was to come next, and after all he never took my credentials. When I got out of the car, I noticed a cross on his collar but I never said a word. He looked at me as a father would look at his child and said, "Listen, when you are driving a car, nothing is more important than what you are doing at that moment. Lives depend on you to be present in the moment, so again I ask you what were you thinking?" All I could do was tell the truth and I told him, "Officer I am going through a lot and I had all manners of insanity going through my head." He immediately told me to stay focused and slow down and the sanity would come." As I got back in the car all I could do was cry because I realized that this was a God thing. As I got down the road I realized there was a serious accident and had I stayed in that mindset, I could very well had been one of the fatalities of that accident. That day, God used that man to be the State Patrol of my Sanity. Who are you allowing to patrol your sanity? Is it emotions, relationships, money, jobs, or family? Whatever it is slow down and stay focused as the father of sanity has already worked it out.

Day 253

SQUIRM BECAUSE I AM NOT SQUASHED

I believe that I have shared with you that as a kid, my brother was a big World Wrestling Federation fan. I hated it because on Mondays, when it went off I knew what was coming next, he was going to try the new moves he saw on me. Many years later, I dated a gentleman who loved wrestling more than my brother did, and he was a Pastor. I told him about how I felt about wrestling when he invited me to go to a wrestling match with him. When I told him, he looked at me and laughed. He went on to tell me why he loved wrestling so much and always has. He told me of how he knew that was a precursor to his calling. He invited me over one night for a surprise. Reluctantly I went. He had the living room set up as though we were going to watch a football game. To my surprise, it was wrestling matches. He asked me to just trust him and watch one match and then tell him what I thought. Reluctantly I did. When we sat down at dinner, he began to ask me questions about the match. As I answered the questions the revelation came flooding my mind. He said, "How do you know when someone is out of the match?" I said, "Because the ref counts to three?" "Exactly, and what does three represent?" He asked. I said, "The Trinity?" "Right again," he stated. I had no idea where he was going with this, but I played along. He then said "What do you notice about when the man is down in the ring and the opponent is on top of him?" I said, "That he's hurt?" He looked at me and told me to go deeper. Right about there I got lost because all I saw was a man down and another one beating the crap out of him and the crowd cheering and in the moment I was having flash backs of what my

505

brother had done to me. He then rephrased the question and said, "If the man on the bottom is still moving, there is a greater likelihood that he can make a comeback and still win the fight then if he just laid there lifeless. Immediately I let out a Holy Ghost shout because I got it. If we can still move when it feels like the enemy is beating the hell out of us, there is a likelihood that our supernatural strength will kick in and we will win, but you got to squirm so you don't get squashed and the people can still see that there is life in you!

FROM DYSFUNCTION TO FUNCTION

It is in our dysfunction that God finds the greatest way to make us functional for the Kingdom. Being functional for the kingdom does not mean that you are flawless. It means that you are honest enough to acknowledge your dysfunction, and then to share it that people may see your dysfunction and be blessed. They are blessed in knowing that your God is also their God, and if he can help you, surely he can help them too. This is the bliss of being honest. Anytime I meet a new person of relationship interest, I always tell them under the unction of the Holy Ghost about my past of homosexuality. Why? Good question! Because it is a part of the platform to which I operate from. I never want them to read my books, or see me minister and be caught off guard about anything from my past. Though it is my past and I am separated and delivered from those entities, that dysfunction is still very much a part of my testimony because it made me who I am today. I have to remember that how they respond is totally up to them, my part is just to be honest about my dysfunction and use it to function for the Kingdom. I dare you today to stop hiding your dysfunction, but stand in it and use it to show the functionality of God's grace and mercy.

I'M PUTTING MY HEAD BETWEEN MY LEGS

It is an interesting fact that when one feels as though they are about to faint, the first thing that the old adage says to do is to put your head between your legs. When you put your head between your legs it causes the blood to flow back to where it needs to be, in the head. Spiritually, when you put your head between your legs you are shutting out what others have to say and think. I call it realigning yourself to the center of your being and allowing the blood of Jesus to re-center your focus. It keeps you from feeling pulled and torn between two or more spectrums; what you want to do, what God wants you to do, and what people have to say about what you are doing. Re-center, refocus, relax, relate, release and reactivate!

In the Anointing and in My Flesh

As a people with prophetic gifts and anointing, we have to be careful that when we speak, we are not speaking from our flesh, but from the Spirit under the direction of the Holy Ghost. I, for one, do not like to minister prophetically to people that I know because I am common to them. I also don't like to do it because I know too much. I am blessed to have a prophetic connection to some people that God will allow them to come around right when I need them to minister to my loved ones and friends. The great thing about integrity and trust is that my friends know that I am not one to tell their business to anyone else, and most of them are also mature enough to decipher the difference between when someone is speaking to them from the throne versus from the "hellophone." This is important and it takes a level of maturity. The anointing will push one to have patience with someone, when the flesh says, "Enough is enough!" The anointing will push one to love past the limits that their flesh has imposed before it gives up on an individual. So when operating, make sure that it is from the spirit in which the anointing operates and not from your flesh. It is a matter of life and death that this happens.

STRIPPING FOR STACKING

I remember when I went through the painful breakup of my first marriage and I moved to Texas with two kids, their clothes and toys and the clothes on my back. My aunt had told me to come home, though I had never lived in Texas she also told me to move in with her. Mind you again that when I left Georgia, all I had was the $301.24 that belonged to the car people, but I chose to use it to break free from the abuse that we were living in. When I got here, I had to make quick money because I had kids to support and I needed to start my life all over. I took on a number of jobs and one of them happened to be stripping. Yep, I did that! Not proud, but I did! I had to strip off my clothes so that I could stack paper to enable me to care for my kids. Though I only performed this act for a season, I remember the ladies there telling me how odd I was and how I didn't belong there. The men would give me money and tell me to stay dressed. All along, I had no idea what God was doing, but now I see it as a revelation for a greater truth. In the worldly realm I was stripping my clothes off, in the spiritual realm; I was stripping my pride away. In the earthly realm, I was stacking my paper, but in the spiritual realm, I was stacking up on my ability not to judge people. What are you stripping away so that God can stack for you! I have learned that in life we all go through a season of spiritual stripping so that God can stack on to you what you need to pursue and be successful in your journey and call. Let it go and let him in!

UNDERSTANDING JUDGEMENT

Whenever we are doing something that we know is contrary to the way and will of the Lord and someone brings it to our attention, the first defense that we use is that they are judging you. For the sake of today's devotional let's explore the definition of judgement.

To judge means to hear (or see) evidence or legal arguments in (a case) in order to pass judgment; adjudicate; try:

Why is this important you ask? Good question! If someone is looking at or hearing your actions and it is contrary to the will and way of the father, they have every right to call you on it and it's not judging you, but it is holding you accountable. I know and I understand what it is like to be held accountable and called to the carpet to stand in something that I am not ready to let go of, but if you survive it, heed to the warning and use better personal judgement, you will be more equipped for use in the Kingdom. Take off the victim's hat and be ye held accountable.

I Don't have the Details, but I'm Coming Out

There are times in our lives where we find ourselves in less than favorable conditions. Sometimes it's in our own doing and other times not so much, but nevertheless, the end result is still the same, tragedy. Large or small a tragedy is a tragedy and a tragedy is always uncomfortable and inconvenient, but the great thing about tragedy is that through God you can and will always come through it. You may not know how, and you may not know when, but you know, that the God of all grace can and will bring your through it. The details of how may be unclear, but you know that he will bring you out! Your hair may be all over your head, but you know that he will bring you out! You may have bumps and bruises from the struggle, but you know that he will bring you out! Stand in that faith and in the liberty that has set you free and tell the world, "I may not have the details to how, but I know that I am coming out!"

IT WAS IN MY FALLING!

There is power in falling! In fact, that is the most likely time when God will and can step in is when you are down. You have used all your knowledge, used all of your intellect and yet and still the problem is still there. It is when you fall into position that he can manifest his glory in your life. It is not only WHEN you fall, but HOW you fall and what you do when you are down there. No matter how you fall if you worship, he will meet you! When you cry out, he will hear you! When you ball up in the fetal position, he will rebirth you to where you won't even know your yourself when you rise. Notice I said, "When you rise." I didn't say IF but WHEN. This is a guarantee that it is going to happen, but you first have to fall.

I SURVIVED!

What I went through didn't kill me,
I survived!
What I went through made me mad,
I survived!
What I went through left me broken, bitter, and disgusted,
I survived!
I survived because God has need of me.
I survived because someone needs to hear my story.
I survived because I was too blessed to die!
I have too much greatness inside of me to die!
I still have a hope and a dream, a calling and a destiny to fulfill
I survived just because!
Go now and SURVIVE to thrive.

Day 262

OUT OF MY COMFORT ZONE!

Many of the blessings that I have received have been out of my comfort zone. Many of the trials that I have endured have been outside of my comfort zone. What is a comfort zone? It is a zone in which you have connections and affiliations to assist you out of a situation. What does that mean? Let me put it like this. I was a military brat. I was born in Oklahoma, lived there til I was eight years old. I then moved to Europe and lived there until I was thirteen. When we left there we moved to Georgia which is where my step dad retired, my mother passed, and my children were born. Now my mother was from Galveston, Texas and my birth father was from Jasper, Texas. It wasn't until I was in my 20's that I decided to move to Texas to get to know my family that I began to establish some roots. I would always marvel at people who had been in the same place all of their life. Born and raised in a certain area. They can point out the schools that they went to and the teachers that they had and they knew all of their high school friends and would attend each other's life occasions like weddings and funerals and the like. I also felt a little irritated because I never really had that fortune. Due to this fact, the blessing is that I never had a real comfort zone. I moved too much. I had the same friends for no more than four years before we moved somewhere else and I had to make more friends. The blessing in that is that my lifestyle made me flexible. I watch my dad, when I tell him that there is something wrong with my car, he says, "Take it to Bubba, he will take care of it." I tell my dad that I need to go somewhere, but I am not sure where it is, he tells me, "Oh around the corner and that place is in the old so and so building." Forgetting that I am not from here, so I don't know about the old so and so building. The reason why I bring this up is because I have noticed that the people who are rooted and grounded in one place have a harder time adjusting to change and leaving their comfort zone, whereas for me it is a way of life. In fact, I think that I have moved just as much as an adult as I did as a child. I'm telling you this because perhaps you are battling making a decision right now. Just be open to the fact that your blessing may be out of your comfort zone!

FROM MINORITY TO MAJORITY AND BACK AGAIN!

Life brings us different scenarios that cause us to have a different status quo in life. In my immediate surroundings as a black woman, I am a majority, yet my education level makes me a minority, then as a single lady, again I am a majority. This pendulum of my life status goes back and forth. When I mentor women and girls, I always tell them that the higher up you go, the lonelier it gets. There are certain things that separate us from the masses, and our personal relationship with Christ should be one of them. To be saved is a minority, to be church going is a majority, to be called is a smaller minority, to have a personal and real relationship with him, the spectrum gets smaller. To be used of God is even smaller, and finally to be formally educated in the Christendom is almost unheard of. Did you know that you can be a majority in the room horizontally, but a minority vertically? All I am saying is don't be afraid of being a minority, and don't be so comfortable being in the majority. Find your path and walk it out!

I HAVE ROOM TO GROW!

As an avid learner and an educator, I am able to thrive in many environments. With that being said, my favorite environment is in one in which I feel like a student. I love to learn and I actually consider it my greatest addiction. Though I am highly educated, I am always seeking the next lesson. The interesting thing is the fact that though I am highly educated, it is common interest that God and I have which is to sit amongst those who are unlearned and learn from them. Jesus became a carpenter and spoke carpentry terms, to the fisher he uses fisherman terms, and to the potter he used pottery terms. This is my ultimate goal, to be as flexible as Christ is, in hopes to be as impacting as he is. See when I sit amongst people with different defined trades, I feel most empowered because I am getting in a few minutes what it took them years to learn. After my encounter with them, I take it back to my toolbox of educational techniques, and I apply it to a lesson after which God breathes upon it and gives me revelation. Most important, it shows me that I will always have room to grow. This is the reason why education, to me, is the most important entity and career choice; because you have to be creative in order to be successful and you have to embrace the opportunity of having room to grow. How committed are you to your growth?

Day 265

YOU LEFT ME FOR DEAD, BUT I AM STILL HERE!

We all have people who glory in our demise. There are those that look for us to fall and feel good when it happens. Those who don't pray for our failure, but they don't pray for our success either! They don't care if we make it, but they are more apt to talk about when we don't! You know the people who tell, you after the storm, how you should have called them and they would have been there, but as soon as the opportunity arises again, they are not available and don't even pick up the phone. These are the people who I say, leave you for dead! Leaving you for dead is not a bad thing because if the cards are played right, yes they will see you fall before their eyes but before the same eyes, they also see God raise you up. They see how God uses you mightily, despite the mess you were in. These people are the Peninah's in your Hannah life. The irritants that God uses to make you want to lay down your religion (if that were possible), and get with them on another level. I have found in my experience that the ones who leave you for dead are the ones that God will use you to minister to in the most intimate way. Notice I said that God will use you, not that you go willingly, not that you and God will never exchange words about the matter, but the fact that he will still use you mightily to speak a word to those people and they will know that it is no one but him operating in your life. The questions are, "Will you make yourself available?" and "Will you be obedient?"

FUNCTIONAL, BUT NOT FINISHED!

It is important for us to realize that just because we are functional does not mean that God is through with us. You can be functional and still not finished. In fact, some of the most powerful sermons that I have preached are the ones that I, myself, was still living. To me, this is the manner in which God keeps us humble. Now, I am in no way saying get up there and be fake and phony, but what I am saying is that when you listen to the voice of God, he will put that thing together in such a way that it is literally a two edged sword helping you and the congregants at the same time. The question is, "Will you be honest enough to say, 'I'm not finished!" Will you be like Paul who said, "Oh wretched man that I am?" Will you be honest enough to say, "I count not myself to have apprehended…!" This is the honesty that the body needs today. Don't talk over the people, get with them and talk to them! Be functional, even though you're not finished!

I LOST IT IN THE STORM

When we encounter storms in our lives, we almost always come out on the other side, seeing ourselves with less than what we started with. This, at times, becomes discouraging and makes us quite indifferent about the situation. Especially when it comes to marriage and relationships, we find ourselves living in the mentality that it is "cheaper to keep her." I, for one, have learned that this methodology is never good. Have I been through storms in my life? Yes! Have I lost somethings, sometimes even myself? Yes! Did I get angry about the situation? Yes! Did I want to retaliate? Yes! But just before my weariness kicked in and my anger turned to sin, God reminded me that it was good for me to lose some things in the storm. At one point, he even had me to sit down and write the things that I lost in the storm. When I got this assignment from the throne, I began to write down what I lost (i.e. cars, houses, money, time…) In the midst of my tangent, he stopped me and said no, start again and think deeper. Make a list of the things you lost and the things you gained as a result. This is what that list looked like;

I lost...	I gained...
A marriage	Myself
A car	Peace of mind
A house	Financial freedom
Pride	Peace
Prejudice	Inclusivity
Job	A Career

All I am trying to say is that it's not about what you lost, but focus on what you gained because none of it can be purchased with money!

STRIPPED, WOUNDED, AND LEFT

I talk a lot in my books about being transparent and being honest and open. I stand by this truth 100%. I believe that it is vitally necessary; however, I will share a word of caution with you. Only share as the spirit leads. The reason for this is because there are and will always be people who will take your story and use it against you. These are what I call "joy stealers!" These are the thieves that the Good Samaritan fell among that stripped him, wounded him, and then they left him. I have never been one to be afraid of sharing my story, however, I had to begin using wisdom as to how, and with whom I should share it with. See there was a time that I shared my story with a "Joy Stealer" and I told it to him in the strictest of confidence, and before I knew it, he had shared it with the congregation and the community. By the time I returned home from tour, the story was distorted, which stripped me of my dignity. It was seasoned with a lot of untruths, which ruined my reputation. Finally, my witness was left for dead (the Bible says, "Half dead"). I didn't see a way through this storm. I didn't even know how to recover, but the half dead part is what blessed me and let me know that because it was half dead, there was still room for God to show himself as strong and mighty as he is. He took that experience and seasoned me with grace, love and most of all liberty. He opened doors where I could tell the truth, and people were able to be blessed by not only my words, but also the actions that I DID NOT TAKE! That was the most powerful testimony of all. So yes, please be honest, yes please be transparent, but also proceed with caution and be sure that you are God led in your sharing.

THEY TOOK MY FIGHT OUT OF ME!

We have all been through our share of storms but there is always that one, that you declare, "God, I don't know if I can make it through this one because they took the fight of me with this." You know the time when the one you trusted the most betrayed you and you said, "I don't have any fight left in me for this!" You know that time you were falsely accused in the midst of another storm, and you decided enough is enough and you said, "I don't have no fight left in me for this!" That time when the child that you nearly died having looks in your face and cusses you out under the influence of the enemy and you just looked up with tears in your eyes and you said, "I don't have no fight left in me for this!" My friends that is when God resurrects the warrior in you. Now you have fight and strength on another level and it reminds you that you can't give up now!

FROM HURTING TO HEALED

I love so many things about God, but one of the things that I love most is his ability to heal the hurting. Most of the time when we mention healing, many people think of infirmities of the body, but how many of us know that many infirmities of the body come from infirmities of the mind! Stress is a mental condition that manifests itself physically in many ways such as headaches and the like. The thing is that many of us would pray the headache away, and never think of the root from which the headache came. Because God is sovereign, he is able to heal at the root of an issue, but he will only heal what you acknowledge. Today, I encourage you to acknowledge your hurts and your pains and don't just pray that God heal the manifestation of a deeper issue, but ask him to heal that thing from the root. This is the difference in being healed and being made whole and when he does it, be sure to be the one to return and tell him thank you!

I Know I Didn't Give You Enough

One of the things that I love about being a member of smaller congregations is that you have more direct access to the Pastor. For some people this is not good because they don't know how to handle it and they become too comfortable with the leadership, but for me it allows me to see the heart of the leaders. Having been in ministry for over 30 years, I know the struggle to reconcile the call of the leaders. I know what it feels like when God didn't give you enough. Not enough time in a day to meet every need. Not enough finances in the church to keep the ministry afloat so you watch the leaders dig into their own personal funds to keep the ministry going. I know what it is to have a big vision and a small congregation. Though I have never been a Pastor, I have assisted enough to witness the struggle. One day I was crazy enough to ask God why did he set the people up that way and his response was as long as they don't have enough they will always lean, depend, and rely on me. This is the thorn in their side. It's when they have more than enough that pride and arrogance steps in both of which I hate. So starting with not enough established their foundation and relationship with me first, and then I will do the adding. So don't be discouraged if you don't have enough, God will bring you the increase.

He Inhabits the Praise,
but He Lives in Your Storm!

There are many times that we go through storms and we ask God where is he? We talk to him as though he is not there, and is oblivious to our struggles and our issues. The Bible clearly tells us that he inhabits the praises of his people, but the problem is that it is hard to praise under pressure. When you are going through your storm, it's hard to raise your hands. When you're going through your storm, at times, it's hard to find a song and a dance. The greatest truth that we often forget is that yes inhabits our praises, but he lives in our storms. We know that because he said that he would never leave us nor forsake us which means that while we are going thru our issues, he is always right there. So know, my friends, that you are never alone. As long as you go through, just know he is never far away.

I SEE YOU TRYING!

Come on, give me a break! Why is it that we expect new converts to operate like seasoned soldiers? Why do we expect them to come in knowing the language and the lingo, exceeding our ever-changing expectations, participating in our Sunday morning? The pressure is overwhelming and the effect is that our church body is dying off. Many people don't go to church for this very reason, they don't get credit for at least trying to change. All of their life, they have been living any kind of way, and we expect them to come in and change immediately when the truth of the matter is that many of us are still struggling with issues after a number of years. I love God, I love church, I love worship, but honestly there are times when I feel like I can deal without the people. As an educator, I have learned that my students are more apt to give me more effort when I celebrate their little victories. Son, I am proud of you because today, I only had to move you once instead of three and four times. Daughter, I am so proud of you for bringing your homework back from last night. I learned that instead of telling them how many problems that they got right, that I tell them hey, today you got three right, I am so excited. What matters is honoring the effort. Acknowledging the energy they are exerting to change. Today, I challenge you to change your language and honor the effort of others.

545

ARE YOU OKAY?

"Mom, I wrecked my car!" she said. "Are you okay?" Mom asked. People feel as though they matter when they hear the simple words "Are you okay?" It is music to my ears when I hear my children call home and say, "Hey Mom, are you okay?" When people ask you that, it shows a level of concern that minimizes the pain in a way one will never be able to understand. It makes people feel as though they matter. It takes away the feeling that we are invisible to people except for the needs that they have of us. It also shows that no matter what people go through, when you ask that question, it subliminally answers the silent questions of what matters most. Even if they say yes, but mean no, just asking increases their ability to share their issues and struggles all because they heard you ask those three words, "ARE YOU OKAY?"

I'M FEARFUL IN SAFE PLACES

We all understand that fear is not of God, but it doesn't stop us from feeling it. Because we shouldn't feel it, doesn't mean that we don't. It is because we operate in humanity that fear exists. Fear is a positive in the fact that it keeps us in reliance on God, and in compliance with God. One of the safest places on earth should be the church. If this is the case, then why is it that we feel fearful in this safe place? Many are fearful because they know what they are doing on the outside and interchanging fear and guilt within themselves on the inside. Perhaps they are fearful in this safe place because they feel as though they cannot live up to the unrealistic expectations of the people in the church. Whatever the reason is, we have to acknowledge that there is a presence of fear within us when we are in what is to be the safe place. Evaluate your worship center today and ask yourself is it a safe place where people feel as though they can make a mistake and not be judged. It is a place where they can ask questions and not be ridiculed. It is a place where they can grow in knowledge and grace. Check it out and make the changes that need to be made to meet the needs of the people, this is the only way that we will grow.

I'M GOING TO HELP YOU HELP ME!

I have talked a lot to the leaders in the church about what they need to do to accommodate the new converts. Today, I am going to talk to the congregants of the church. You cannot expect for your leader to know what it is that you need if you don't communicate the need. You have to be able to help them help you. Just like babies don't come with instruction books neither do churches and ministries. In my first book entitled Churchin' Ain't Easy I tell people how to go from religion to relationship. I even cover how to find a church home. If I had it to do over again, I would add a chapter with the title of this devotional. I think that we, as members, don't empower our leaders enough about the matters which are important to us. Then when they make decisions that seem not to include us, we get upset and want to leave or we murmur and complain. Help your leaders help you by articulating what it is that you feel you need help in. If they don't have anything formal in place, ask them is it possible to maybe create something. Help them help you!

I'm Not Wasting My Time!

We are living in such a time where we don't have time to waste. We have to live intentional. We have to move with purpose. We have to operate with passion. Many of us can safely say that we have more days behind us than in front of us. With that in mind, we have to purpose in our hearts and minds to be about the fathers business and honor it accordingly so that we are making the most beneficial use of our time in relation to the kingdom. There is no time to waste over petty matters as to who is preaching when, who is teaching when, who is singing what song and who is playing what instrument. We have to operate in urgency to ensure that no one is left behind when Christ cracks the sky!

I'M TOO VALUABLE!

You are too valuable to give your extraordinary self to any ordinary person. You are too precious to be pressured to be something that you are not. You are too loved to be locked into a relationship that is not healthy, not befitting to produce the best you! You are too honored to be looking for something or accepting someone who doesn't know your worth. You are too revered to be disrespected by people who should feel blessed just to be in your presence. I don't think that, as a people, we hear enough just how valuable we are to God. I think that we take it lightly when we are told that we are made in his likeness and image. So many scriptures speak to us about how important we are, but there are so many forces that tell us otherwise. We have to be careful of how we operate and who we operate with. Connections can kill your witness quicker than any act that you can perform. Know your worth, know your value and proceed with caution.

MY DEPOSIT IS TOO GREAT!

We learned yesterday about how valuable we are and now today we have to address the value of the deposits that we make into people. I have to ask, if you know a person that is in any form of riotous living such as drugs and alcohol and they came and asked you for money for food, would you be more apt to feed them or would you just give them your hard earned cash? If we be honest, many just ignore these people all together for many reasons, but then then there are those like me who say, "I would get them some food and take it to them." If they decline, you know what their motive was to begin with, but you don't wallow in their decline. Your conscious is clear that you done the God thing of extending, but it was theirs to accept or reject. If we can make this kind of conclusion or resolution for this matter, why can we not make this same resolution in other scenarios of our lives? Your spiritual deposits are more valuable than your financial deposits, so why do we keep giving ourselves away to people who don't appreciate us? Why do we keep reaching out to people who are unaware of just how valuable our deposits are? Someone once said that imitation is the greatest form of flattery. I beg to differ. I remember one time hearing a preacher tell me that he wanted my sermon notes and all of my props because he was going to re-preach my message, as a lot of his members were not present for the occasion. I laughed it off until I realized that he was serious. Immediately I was alarmed because that, to me, spoke of the lack of time that he gives to God to receive his own word and revelation. I immediately told him that the price of this word was too costly for imitation. Whether he got what I was saying or not, I don't have a clue, but what he did do was stop asking for it. Honor your deposits not only that you make, but the deposits that God makes into you and operate in a manner that is pleasing to God.

Day 280

SERVING NO PURPOSE BRINGS CURSES

One of the things that I have noticed about small, and even some large, churches is that when the members are idle there is where the mess begins. I would often wonder why, and then it was revealed that when their hands are idle, so are their minds. No purpose brings about curses. Cursed is the body that has members with idle hands. Why? Because this is when the murmuring and complaining begins. This is when the strife and division comes in. They begin to look at the active ones as though they are doing something wrong and then they began to do a lot of fault finding, they start the rumor mills, and before you know it they become the cancer that destroys the church body. What shall we say then? Get their interest and keep them busy with productive Kingdom work!

YOU ARE ATTRACTIVE!

Being in the forefront brings about a level of attraction. Beyoncé is more attractive because of her position and what she possesses. If she were not in the spot light, she would be just another beautiful woman amongst the rest of us in day to day life. I had to learn that as an author, speaker, preacher, professional, entrepreneur, singer, preacher and much more that all require some time in the spotlight brings about a level of attraction that can mean death to those who are not sober and vigilant to the tactics of the enemy. See when you are in the limelight there is another level of warfare that takes place that makes one attach to you for the light and not the love. They are there as long as you are in the light, but when the light goes down they change. Sooner or later they try to dim your light to promote their own. You are attractive! You are attractive for the level of anointing that you possess! You are attractive because the level of knowledge that you have. There are so many things that can attract people to you and it has everything to do with their motive. You just have to be sober and vigilant and be able to discern the spirit and ask for direction as to who you are supposed to connect with and why.

Day 282

TALK TO ME!

Talk to me,
Not the image of me that you see!
Talk to me,
Tell me your plan and purpose for our life together as you see it
Talk to me,
Not at me, because they greatness that I possess supersedes any other mess.
Talk to me,
So that you may see all of God's blessings that are within me!
Talk to me,
I need to hear from you, I need a word that will help bring me through.
A word that will speak to my core,
A word that I can never ignore,
A word that can realign my DNA,
A word that will leave me without words to say.
Talk to me God,
I am listening every so intently.
Just speak a word and I know it will pierce me ever so gently.

NEVER!

Did I ever think anyone could love me like you?

Never!

Did I ever think that anyone could find value in me the way that you did?

Never!

Did I ever believe that I would be doing half of the things that you have graced me to do?

Never!

Never in a million years would I believe that someone would invest so much in me and trust me, even in the midst of my mess.

Nevertheless, God I just want to say thank you for how far you have brought me, how much you have taught me. If I could just see myself half as valuable as you see me, it is less likely that I would find myself settling for less than the best that you have for me. I love you with all that is within me. If ever you asked me the question will I ever leave you, despite all that I have to go through, my answer would be Never!

Day 284

BALANCE IS THE NAME OF THE GAME!

Balance is when you understand that you are a spiritual being living in a human world.

Balance is when you realize there are a number of hats that one must wear to be everything to everyone, but at the end of the day, you still have to find a way to invest in yourself!

Balance is where you spend enough time in the word to be fueled, but also enough time in the world to be effective.

Balance!

Imbalance comes with a price of burnout until you find your place of stability in your ability to be all things to all people that someone may run to Christ saying, "What must I do to be saved?"

Balance is understanding that, after God, I have to be the first priority on my list because if I have not made enough deposits in myself and/or allowed others to make deposits into me, yet I give of myself, I will only find myself on spiritual overdraft, mental burnout and emotionally bitter and anguished. There is a method to the madness that is my life; I just have to remain balanced to see it for what it is.

IT'S DANGEROUS!

It is dangerous to place gifts in the hands of carnal people. It is dangerous to expect more from a person than they are able to give. It is dangerous to try to be someone you are not, to please someone you don't know, to express emotions that you don't show, or more so to teach a lesson you have not learned. It is dangerous! It is dangerous, as a leader, to place people in positions that they are not equipped for and expect them to be effective. The reality is that they will become the serpent that spits venom into the lives of the people because instead of speaking a word, they speak and show motive for all to see. Look out for the danger, and proceed with caution. Lives are on the line!

GOD DIDN'T SAVE YOU FOR THAT!

God didn't save you to create a platform for you!

He didn't save you to make a stage out of your life!

He didn't save you for you to market yourself as someone's spiritual superhero!

He didn't invest gifts and talents into you to feed your ego or for you to try to trump up superhero spiritual games of chess with people's lives.

He didn't save you so that he can equip you with gifts that make people see more of you and less of him. I declare that is not what he saved you for. He didn't mean for you to become arrogant or self-righteous. He didn't educate you for the sake of your "bigness." It is not about you! Not about your gifts, talents and/or be recognized. It is all about him and him alone. Your gift will take you where your character cannot keep you! Beware! The heart of the matter is God!

ASSISTANCE FOR THE RESILIENCE

Resilient people are the ones who take a licking and keep on ticking! They fall, but they also get up. They put forth effort to beat the odds that have been spoken against them. They are the ones who wait patiently in line for the great exchange of God. This is the great exchange where he makes the last first, and the first last. This is the great exchange where he gives you beauty for ashes. The people who know that weeping endures only for a night, but when morning comes, God is going to exchange their weeping for joy. These are the people whom God is ever ready to assist. These are the people who do not eat sorrow sandwiches when things don't go their way, they don't sit around feeling sorry for themselves, not wondering when it will be my turn. No, they stay on their face before God waiting for their change to come believing by faith that it will be sooner than later. There is assistance for the resistance based on their faith alone. It is based on their tenacity that says, "God no matter what, I still trust you!" "If you don't answer the prayer right now, it doesn't mean that you can't, it just means that the timing is not right, but until you do, I will wait." It is when God sees that level of love, devotion, and confidence that he moves on their behalf. Be resilient so that he can bring your assistance, but you have to act first.

ITS' JUST THAT SIMPLE

We, as believers, make being a Christian so difficult. We fill people with all these rules, traditions, and methodologies. We make it so complex with our ability to half way interpret Greek and Latin, and we dissolution people with our knowledge and make them feel like these matters are a requirement. Can we get back to the basics that say, "There are two simple principles that one must follow to be a Christian and that is to love God and to love people." Nowhere in there does intellect and translations, head coverings and attire, forbidden colors and jewelry come into play. Our only requirement is to love God and love people. In my classroom, I use a well know acronym known as K.I.S.S. in this case it means Keep It Simple Saints! It will increase the Kingdom at a rapid rate.

Day 289

FORMED, FILLED, FUNCTION

There is a simple continuum for Christendom that is literally a three step process. God formed us in his image, and then he filled us with his Holy Ghost to empower others through our functioning. He called you to function. Function in whatever capacity you are able to effectively operate. By doing this, you are able to bring others in on the cyclic function of Christendom: to be formed, filled, and then to function.

I THOUGHT I FAILED WHEN I FELL!

We have all fallen at one point or another in our lives. I can't speak for you, but when I fell, I felt that I was at my lowest point. I didn't see that it was in my falling that God empowered me the most. When I fell, that was when I was most apt to hear him speak. I fell below the line of the noise. I couldn't hear what people were saying. It didn't matter to me anymore what they thought, after all their opinions were a part of the contributing factors to my fall. Please let me be the one to encourage you that there is no failure in falling; it is just a position of surrender where no one but God can get the glory out of the situation.

DON'T PRESERVE THE TEMPORARY

We spend so much time trying to preserve the temporary dwelling in which we live, our bodies. How much time, energy and finances do we invest in weaves, lifts, tattoos, false this, lifting that and tucking this. Imagine how powerful it would be if we invested and equal amount of time in our spiritual walk and talk. What if we spent half the time that we spend on beauty methods reading our word or praying, how much more powerful, effective, and fit to function would we be? Instead we choose to take these measures to invest in the mere shell in which we live: the shell that will be left behind in the rapture. I dare you to keep this thought in your perspective as you go through your daily life and see just what it is that God makes most important in his word. Never once did I read where he talked about arched eyebrows and natural versus permed hair. Not once did he mention the sanctified fashion shows that we all take part in on Sunday mornings. No, God only mentions the heart because that is what he deals with, the heart of man. Stop taking so much time trying to preserve the temporary and invest in the eternal.

I HAD TO COME TO MYSELF

The longest trip in the Bible was when the Prodigal son came to himself. This is a story that we all know, whether we are churched or unchurched, saved or unsaved, delivered or in bondage. We are all familiar with the story of the prodigal son. Not only is it the longest traveled trip of the Bible, but it is also the most shared, and the most relatable story in the Bible because it is a road that we all must travel down at some point or another in our lives. Coming to ourselves is the hardest trip to make because there are so many odds that are against us. We have to tread down the road of loneliness and look past the forest of desperation. We have to lose our hearing of others to concentrate on the still, small voice that is Christ. It is a place where we have to go through the obstacles of life only to discover that we really have no clue where we are going or what we are really doing. In reality we have to lose ourselves in him only so that he can help us to find ourselves. This is how we are developed in him. This is how we grow in him. This is how our virtues and our fruits are made manifest because we are so enveloped in him that our own agendas don't even matter. Lose yourself in him only so that you may find yourself. It will all be worth it.

HE DOESN'T RECOGNIZE YOU!

Many of us walk through life looking for a blessing from a man who refuses to bless a stranger that he doesn't recognize. Yes, he knows you by name, he even knows the hairs on your head, but he doesn't recognize the you that you have chosen to become: the superficial you, the one with the masks and the falsities that come from the pits of hell. He cannot see the you that he created because you have camouflaged it with worldly desires and techniques that you think make you look and feel better, but you never consulted him to see how he felt about the matter. You never delight yourself in him anymore so that he can give you the desires of your heart. He doesn't see the authentic creation that he made in his likeness and in his image; he only sees who you are pretending to be. Find the authenticity of who you were created to be so that he can recognize and bless you.

COMPASSION FATIGUE

Most marriages fail after a catastrophic occurrence. Some friendships cannot survive the neediness that comes after tragedy. People who are gives often become fatigued in their compassion because they find themselves constantly giving only to be left broke and broken while the ones whom they have helped have gotten what they needed and moved on forgetting the ones who was there for them. There is nothing more painful than feeling used and abused. There comes a time when this occurs so often that many people with great hearts actually wax cold and become desensitized to the needs of others because they no longer have the desire to assist with compassion. They feel that they know how the story is going to end. If we be honest, we will all come to this fork in the road where we have to decide whether to help and be left or to not help and see how long the relationship lasts. I have found myself in this place, but I have resolved to still keep trying and believing God for the increase to be returned to me one hundred fold. Not because that is why I do it when I bless others, but because it's in my fatigue that he makes me more fruitful.

STORMS COME TO TEST YOUR FOUNDATION

I remember when I was talking to a contractor about the possibility of building a home. I was stuck between the options of buying or building and I wanted his expert opinion about each. He began to talk to me about ensuring that the house has a good foundation. He went on to say that the perk of buying an older home is that it has been through prior storms and had survived the possibility of foundation issues as well as shift. He continued saying that in building a home you can only speak in theory of the security of the foundation. It would and could not be proven effective until it endured its first storm. Of course you know the baby inside of me leaped when he said that because the same is true for our walk with Christ. You are not proven to be fit until you have endured a storm a two. What happens to you when the wind and the waves come into your life? Will you go into your fight or flight mechanism and if so which will you do? Will you stand and fight for the new right that you know to be true or will you become a flight risk to the local body and leave at the first sign of not getting your way? Even when we enter into relationships you will know the fate of the relationship when a storm hits. As the old adage says, "Time will tell!"

THE PURPOSE OF SPIRITUAL PRENATAL CARE

Just as in a natural pregnancy, prenatal care is vital for the development of the child as well as the health and well-being of the mother. So it is in the spiritual realm. In the world of Christendom, we are always birthing things. In fact, God impregnates us with purpose before we are even born. We walk around impregnated with purpose that cannot be birthed until you are in the right position. The position, meaning you are in right standing with God. You are in a place where your baby can be fed and nourished with the proper ingredients. Yes, you will have to watch your environment because your baby can be infiltrated with infection. You also have to watch the way that you live personally, because for a safe delivery you purpose needs a sterile environment at home as well. Get in the right position and protect your baby at all costs.

Day 297

TIME

Time is an entity that can work for or against us. No matter whether you vote for against time it is still precious. If time was in a campaign, it may look a little something like this;

Vote FOR time! It heals all wounds. Inside of it comes growth and maturity. In the right hands and contexts, it can be quite profitable and can establish a level of comfort and confidence. Vote for time, she can really work in your favor.

No for time! It exposes what needs to be hidden. It ages you beyond belief. It reveals your shortcomings. It's quite impatient and waits for no one. Time…use it or lose it!

What's your vote?

I THREW IN THE TOWEL, AND HE THREW IT BACK!

I threw in the towel because I was tired,
He threw it back and said, "So was I."
I threw in the towel because I was frustrated,
He threw it back and said, "I know the feeling!"
I threw in the towel because I felt betrayed,
He threw it back and said, "Remember Peter?"

What am I saying? What is he saying? We are saying it happens to all of us where we just want to throw in the towel for many reasons. The truth of the matter is that those feelings can be very valid, but now is not the time to neither give up nor throw in the towel. There is too much invested in you!

WHAT I WOULDN'T GIVE FOR A DO OVER?

Aren't you glad we don't serve a God of just a second chance? To be honest, we would have blown that a long time ago, then what? What about all the other times we messed up? I'm so glad that we serve a God of a do over. He gives us chance after chance after chance. Now this is not a scheme to stay in the bondage of sin, but it is a place of grace that says, "I love you my child, now let's get it right!" Thank you God for letting me do some things over.

I THOUGHT IT WAS DARK!

I thought it was dark and no one could see,
I thought the only person who would know was me.
I thought I could hide it,
I would never tell that I laid beside it,
I surely can't say that I invited it!

See exposure has its own light,
When the beam hits it, the truth you can't fight!
Look in its eye,
No one can ever deny
Of how the will of God you defy for a good time and a sigh.

Relief?
Relief you say?
Was it worth the price you had to pay?
Pay it now or pay it later,
Darkness can sneak up and bite you like a gator.
Quickly approaching in the still of the night,
Biting, nibbling, teasing,
None of it is right.
One thing leads to another
Neither light nor darkness matters
With sin don't even bother!

DON'T JUST SIT THERE, DO SOMETHING

1 Corinthians tells us of the many gifts that are within the body. If this be the case, why do so many people sit around idly? There is so much work to do, so many jobs to be done. Don't just sit there, do something. Christendom is more than tithes and offerings; it is about the part of the body that you are called to. You were called because you are fit to function. Young or old, large or small, the charge that you have will benefit us all. There is no little I's and big T's, we all have our weight to pull because the body has needs. Come on get busy, it's not like you don't have time. You sit at home and let the devil speak to your idle mind. When he speaks to your mind, it's not long before it gets to your heart. So exercise you gift, now when can you start?

Day 302

SECRETS OF A SOLD OUT SAINT

There is a not so secret to the sold out saint. They don't do things to be seen. As a matter of fact, it is all because they just want to see the king. They don't need you to know who they blessed and how. They just need you to know that they intend to grow somehow. They are subtle in their actions, but bold in their faith. They are subordinate in their actions, and don't do anything for fame. They are successful in their endeavors because their motive is always clear. They don't need vain glory because they understand that Christ second coming is near.

Day 303

THERE IS A WAR GOING ON!

Did you know that there is a war going on? Yes, and you are the primary target. The devil wants you bad. Yes, there is a war going on but as in everything else, God will not leave you out there on the limb alone. He gives us a strategy. He first wants you to know your enemy. No, it is not each other, in fact the enemy is not flesh and blood at all, but it is principalities, which means that it is all spiritual that manifests itself in the flesh of yourself and others. God also wants you to know all of the tools that the enemy uses, the major one being temptation. Most importantly he wants you to know who your ally is; the one who is really on your side through it all and that is Jesus Christ himself. He is the only one who can articulate your feelings when you can't. He is the only one who can interpret your groan when words seem insufficient. He has your back and the fight is fixed. You are going to win!

Day 304

SEEING WITHOUT SIGHT!

Faith calls for us to see God without sight. The Bible says that faith is the substance of things hoped for, the evidence of things not seen. When we look at the revelation of it, what does it mean? It means that you are able to see without sight! You are able to see God in any obstacle that you have. You are able to see God through whatever opposition you must face. You are able to see him when you are in a bad place and position and when your priorities are a little misguided. You are able to see him when the traffic of the body is moving while you are standing still. You are able to see how to survive when all odds are against you. Most importantly you are able to see how the Savior is going to use this instance, this situation, and circumstance in your life to work for your good. You are able to see him in the spirit, praying for you while you are yet even in your mess. That is what faith is. Seeing without sight!

WHEN THE ANSWER HAS A QUESTION!

What do you do when the answer (Jesus Christ) has a question himself? I love reading the story of the trials and tribulations that Jesus went through prior to his death, especially when he was on the cross. I love it not because it's a great story with a happy ending, but because it shows me not only how much he loves me, but also how much he can really relate to what I am going through. He understands when I gave my all and I have cried and prayed and prayed and cried and still haven't gotten an answer to the questions that I asked. I rejoice in the fact of knowing that he feels my pain when he cried out, "My God, My God, what hast thou forsaken me?" Identify with this story. You don't have to wait for the resurrection season to know that he loves you enough to identify your suffering. Celebrate it now.

NOT THIS TIME!

Paul was a remarkable man who gave us lots of lessons to learn. One of the many important lessons is the call of the thorns in his side. Why do I call it a "Call" of thorns? Because I believe that anything that God uses for a purpose is called for the point and purpose of him getting the glory. The thorns in Paul's side were called for three reasons. One was to conquer pride. Have you ever just known that you could do a thing well? Like you could do it with your eyes closed and then one day something happens that breaks down that ease, or shall we say that spirit of pride? This is done for the sake of the second reason which is to cause you to pray. See pride is when you no longer rely on God, but on your own strength to do a thing and God uses the thorns to keep you relying on him. Finally, the third reason that God called the thorns is to channel your praise to him and not to yourself. It keeps you leaning and depending on him at all times and knowing that in and of yourself you can do nothing, but it is only through him. When you realize that then you are more free to praise him, you know that he and he alone is worthy and not you. So thank God for the times that he said "no." That "no" is the thorn in your side to keep you humble and relying solely on him.

WALK IN YOUR VICTORY!

When you realize that you are victorious in and over every situation, you come to mature in your relationship with Christ. Time always makes us more secure in the relationship that we have not only in him, but with others as well. Over time you come to know the character of the people with whom you are involved. When you walk in victory, it doesn't come overnight, but keep on moving because it will come. It is not saying that you won't ever have moments of doubt, but it is saying that as you walk, you will walk with courage, the courage to face any obstacles that come your way. You will walk in confidence, knowing that if he did it before, he will do it again. Finally you will walk in comfort, knowing that if no one cares about you, Christ does, and it is only in him that you live, move, and have your being, just get to walking and the rest will come.

How to Get Your Joy Back

Do you ever get to a point where you just fall into a dark place? Perhaps if the truth be told, there are times where you throw yourself in a dark place due to your own disobedience. It's ok. It happens to the best of us, and is guaranteed for the rest of us. What do you on those days when you don't want to get out of bed? You are so depressed that you can't eat, you barely sleep? Yep, I knew it because I have been there too. How do you get your joy back? You begin to see life through God's eyes. You let this mind be in you that is in Christ Jesus. Yep, that's it, it's just that simple!

WHY AM I STILL HERE?

Many of us ask the question, "God, why am I still here?" We know
what we have done and we know that we are undeserving. We know that
though we may know some, he knows all and that makes matters even
more baffling. This what God revealed to me when I asked this question.
He said that he retained me here on earth because his name in on the line.
If I died in the midst of my mess, I could not be an example of his grace nor
his mercy. He said that he refrained from giving me what I deserve because
others who see will think that perhaps his grace is not sufficient. He said I
am still here because he wanted to show his glory in the ways that the fire
of life has refined me. Not only that, but I am also here to reveal, not only
his glory, but also to live out the story that shows what I am really made of.
Lastly, you are still here because he restricted the power of the enemy to
ensure that you are successful. He knew the entire time that you are built
to last, not to break, so no more questions just rejoice at the fact that you
are still here!

ACCEPTING WHAT GOD ALLOWS!

One of the hardest tasks of a Christian is accepting what God allows. This means not questioning him, not second guessing him, just walking through life in full acceptance of the fact that you understand that he knows what is best. When you accept what God allows, you take on the mentality to keep progressing. You understand that every test and every trial takes you to a new place in him. You keep the peace because you understand that in the midst of everything that he will give you peace that passeth all understanding and it will guard your heart and your mind. Most importantly, it allows you to keep hope in the promises of God. This means that you understand that defeat doesn't complete a man, but quitting does.

Day 311

THE SERENITY OF THE SECRET PLACE

He that dwelleth in the secret place has not only serenity, but they are opening themselves to the opportunity for God to do a new thing in their thought processes. The power of the thought pattern is transformed in the secret place. There is a throwing out of the old mindset, and then there is an intake of positivity that replaces the old. Whatsoever a man thinketh, so is he. So when you begin to intake the positive then the output will match. This means that you carry out positive actions. How does this happen? I'm glad you asked. You go through three time zones of Christianity. There is the time of Thanksgiving. There is the time of thought provoking positivity and finally a time of renewed trust. You can't help in the still of the day, but to sit back and thank God for all the times when you thought that you wouldn't and couldn't make it. This forces you into a place of positivity and gratefulness and forces you into a new place of trust in him. In the secret place is a time of refreshing, recovering, and revival. Get into the secret place today and watch God work!

THE CRY OF THE RAM

We are all familiar with the ram in the bush, but many of us fail to look at things from the ram's perspective. We talk about Abraham, We talk about Isaac, and we talk about all of the artifacts that they took with them, but let's look at it from a different approach: from the ram's perspective. What would have happened to the ram had Abraham been disobedient? What would have happened to the ram had Abraham dragged his feet after getting instruction from God? The revelation of the cry of the ram is that someone (a ram) is out there waiting for you to help them out of their mess. They are not worried about the number of Bible verses that you know and do not know. They are not worried about the car that you drive. They don't care how long you been in church, how you look, feel, or even your status quo. They just want you to speak to them and their situation, and be honest enough to tell them how you got out and stay out of the thicket so that they might do the same. Lives are on the line waiting for you. How long will you make them wait?

THE TRIAD OF SPIRITUAL FREEDOM

There are three things that form the triad of Spiritual Freedom. There is your PRAISE that makes you stand out. The PRESSURE that is applies to you that make God stand up and the DELIVERANCE that unifies the two. Have you ever been in a worship service, which due to the time constraints and opinion of man that the praise and worship is cut off right in the midst of God's glory trying to reign supreme in the house. I have, and man does it really break my heart. It's like waving meat in the face of a wolf. That is how aggressive I am about worship. Listen, we have to understand that God does not like for his praise to be interrupted, and he's very protective of his own. So if the triad is the pinnacle of freedom when you break the triad of its praise, then how can deliverance take place. The next time that you are involved with praise and worship, especially if you are a leader, I want you to think of this analogy. Somebody is depending on you!

THE SIGNIFICANCE OF THE ONE

We are all familiar with the story of the ten lepers that God healed, but only one came back to give thanks and was made whole. There is revelatory symbolism that takes place in the midst of this story. The leprosy of the story is sin, the priest of the story is the world inspecting you, the nine others are your family, friends and foes, but that ONE should be you! You should be the one who comes back to say thank you! You should be the one who is different in your family. They are healed, but you are whole. This means the generational curse stops with you. You should be the one who shows the difference when the world acts as the priest and examines your life only to declare you unclean, by its standards. You are significant. You matter. You are the one in whom he is well pleased. Go ahead and praise him!

Day 315

DON'T CURSE THE SIFTER!

In our lives, there comes a point where we must go through the sifter, and the sifter is a place of uncertainty. You know that you must go inside of it, but you are just not sure how it's all going to turn out in the end. You know that the promise is going to work out for your good, but it's just that uncertainty and fear of the turbulence that has your stomach in knots. What normally happens when one goes through the sifter? They are separated from all things that they feel like they need like people, places, habits and the like. The sifter is where God does the separating of the tares and the wheats in your life. The sifter is where you go in as friends, but you may come out as enemies, not because they are bad or you are bad, but because, there is a shifting that is taking place and perhaps you all are assigned to grow apart and go your separate ways. So don't curse the sifter because it really is your friend.

Day 316

THINGS THAT I AM **SURE** ABOUT!

There are many uncertainties in life that we go through and many things that we may be unsure about. Salvation should never be one of them, but it is the one thing that the enemy plays on. I have been saved since I was a young child, but I still at times struggle with it. How do I fight this? Every time someone else walks through the sinner's prayer, I do it with them. It doesn't make me any less a Christian, but it just tells him that above all and anything else I want to be sure. Now, I can say with assurance that there are three things that I am sure about; one, Jesus is the Christ, two, I'm his sheep and lastly that I will spend eternity with him! Make sure that you can say the same declaration!

THE BENEFITS OF PRAISE!

You have heard me express my passion for praise and worship several times in this book. Today, I am going to tell you the benefits of that passion. There are things that I get from God every time I praise him. God grants me direction. He tells me exactly where I need to go in reference to decisions that I have to make, be it personal, professional or even in relation to the Kingdom. God grants me deliverance when I praise him. Praise solidifies my belief that he will give me all that I need to make it through my current storm. God grants me durability when I praise him. He lets me see my own strength in him and him alone. In that same vein, he grants me confidence in him. When I praise him, I see it as yet another way to consummate my relationship with him. Why do you praise him?

Day 318

WAIT!

Why is it that it seems in our times of desperation that God makes us wait? Sometimes it honestly feels like a punishment, but I promise there is always a method to the madness of this kind. Why does he tell us to wait when we need him to move most? One reason is to construct Christ like character. He wants to make sure that there is no room for arrogance or the misconception that you did a thing on your own. Another reason is to correct convoluted perceptions of one's self. Sometimes when we are able to do or fix a thing on our own, we have a tendency of encouraging God to take a break on this one. We have twisted ideas that we don't need him this time, and we invite him to help others when we ourselves really need him. Finally, it is to cause calculated celebration. Frustration has a way of setting in when God does not allow for a thing to happen when we think that he should. We have a tendency of holding our breath and just believing him to do it. When he finally comes through, there is a combustion of praise that is calculated, but not premeditated. So don't get weary in your waiting, there is a method to the madness.

Day 319

How Could You?

When we are in the will of God, there is a shifting that takes place that leaves one to think that we have changed or that we have arrived. We know that this is not true; we just answered a call to something greater. We have to be mindful of the actions that people commit when we are truly sold out to God because if you are not prepared it will make you take your eyes off of him. One thing that they will do is sell you out. They will begin gossiping and trying you by your prior life before Christ. They will set you up to see if you have really changed or if this is just a façade. We have to be careful in this phase because they are literally waiting for you to snap just so they can say, "See, I knew you wasn't saved....look how you acting!" Finally, they will let you down. They will build you up in a place, and praise you in your face, but then they turn around and say otherwise to others. I want to encourage you my friends, Jesus went through the same thing, so don't be discouraged. He made it through to show you that you can too.

DON'T QUIT!

We all want to quit at one time or another. We feel like what is the use. People quit for different reasons. One is just the fact that they are pitiful. They came into this place with the desire to not complete the task. They didn't believe in themselves from the beginning. Another reason why people quit is because they are in prestigious positions and they feel like they would rather not even try for fear of failing in the public eye. Finally, another reason that they quit is due to personal problems like the proclamations made to them at some point in time. Well, I came to tell you that there are solutions for not quitting. God made a promise that he would never leave you, nor forsake you. He promised to protect you against every wicked thing that tries to consume you. He also promised provision, so yes, you may be limited in your own strength, but you are able to make it through if you just trust him. Finally, he is putting you in a position where you are successful, but he gets the glory. So, quitting is not an option!

Day 321

THE OTHER SIDE OF SUCCESS

We all want to be successful but there are number of ugly truths about success that many fail to realize, and because they are ill equipped when they see the other side they act adversely. See success is not just about you, but it telegraphs truths about others. Brace yourself for what I am about to say! Not everyone wants to see you successful! Success also has a way of tormenting others around you. We call this modern day "hating." They become insecure, insoluble and intimidated. Know that this has nothing to do with you. Success also makes you a target. The higher you go the more effort others will impose on keeping you down. This is proof of how success turns acquaintances into adversaries. They are not for you fully, but they are also not fully against. This is where the prostitution of your gifts comes. All in all, just beware and know that success ain't always fair, but God's favor is.

STARTING ALL OVER AGAIN!

There is nothing wrong with starting all over again, but there are some precautions that one must take. Starting over is not just about you, but also about the people that are connected to you! Be careful that you don't go backwards. Be careful that guilt doesn't make you flee from the Lord. If you stop running, he will bless you. When you stand still, he takes you through an internal investigation. He will come to you, since you won't come to him. Keep in mind though that he is a gentleman, and that he won't rape you of your will. You still have the final say. When you start all over again, he will also clarify your purpose in spite of. Remember, nothing has changed because you messed up, however, take your time, and be honest about what bothers you. This intervention prevents you from making the same mistake again.

INTERIM OF BLESSING

There is a period of wait time in between blessing and burdens. During this period, God is very strategic of what happens. When you are in between blessings and burdens, you are forced to seek someone bigger. You also get into a position of praise, which dispenses all doubts. The interim between blessings and burdens is all about actively waiting on the manifestation of God in the matters at hand. Just know that in the meantime and in between time, there is activity going on in the heavenlies, even when you can't see it.

TAKING THE BITTER WITH THE SWEET

When the children of Israel came to Marah, which means bitter, they had just crossed the Red Sea. Naturally, they were thirsty from the journey. They asked Moses what they were supposed to drink. Accommodations were made for them in the end, but we want to talk about what happens in the meantime when you are your place of Marah, bitterness. First, you have a prayer meeting. Your place of bitterness is where your prayer life is perfected. Next, you pass the interrogation. This is the place where you commune with God, and you ask him all the questions you want. Though many people say not to question God, there is no biblical reference for that, but there are several instances where God was questioned, even by Jesus himself. Next, you have to literally listen to hear what God says. Finally you accept the Lord's accommodations. This is where you reconcile your actions with the will of God. It won't be easy, but take the bitter with the sweet and keep on moving.

BREAKUP, BREAKDOWN, BREAKTHROUGH!

There are times in our lives where the Lord will breakup strongholds in our lives to free us from the bondages of sin. Because these elements are just what they are called, strong holds, when they are broken up, it causes one to break down, sometimes literally. Why is this you ask? Good question! Because breaking up stronghold takes one out of their comfort zones, out of the elements that they have become accustomed to. When this happens, one is left feeling vulnerable and alone. Their surroundings seem new, their friends are few, and their ability to cope becomes limited. This is the valley of decision where you can decide to breakdown or breakthrough. **B**reakthrough are for the mature saints that says no matter what I go through, I am determined to come through this shining bright like a diamond that was lost in the rough of my mess. The choice is yours! Will you breakup, breakdown or breakthrough.

YOU KNOW WHERE I COME FROM;
GOD KNOWS WHERE I AM GOING!

It is always interesting to see people's perspective of you when God changes you. People look at the actuality of what you used to be, and they even try to discredit who God has called you to be. It's what I call, "Judging you on the actuality of who you used to be and not the anointing that you are now walking in." They have a tendency to look at you in the natural, when God looks at you in the supernatural and does supernatural things in your life that he may get the glory of the change that has taken place in your life. So don't get discouraged when people look at you through their natural eyes and try to cast judgement based on your past, remember that's where you've been, not where you are going.

Day 327

TWO SIDES TO EVERY COIN!

The great thing about God is that he will use you despite the folly of man's opinion. There will always be people who are for and against you. Look at the life of Joseph. He was favored by his parents, but hated by his siblings. He was favored by Potiphar, but hated by Potiphar's wife; so much so, she set him up for a fall. We have to understand that this is a part of life. Not everyone is going to sing your praises all the time, and if they do, you may want to beware because there just may be a snake or two in your camp.

CHANGE IS NOT IN ME, BUT IN HIM!

We try to change in and of ourselves, but we always fail. Why? It is because we try to do it on our own. Though we may start strong, our success in not consistent because our spirit is willing, but our flesh is weak. This means that as much as we may want to change, we cannot do it with God.

THE VALLEY IN BETWEEN MOUNTAINS

Though it would be great to experience only the mountaintop, it is utterly impossible to do. In order to go from one mountain to another, one must come down and experience a low valley. This is just a way of life. When we look at Paul, he told us that he knows what it is to be abase, and to be abound. This means he knows what it is to have and not to have. What it means to be successful versus what it means to not succeed at a thing. We too must have this same understanding. This is the mentality that we all must have. If you can find contentment in whatever state that you are in, then you will have a much easier time bouncing back after a fall. Learn to enjoy the ups as well as appreciate the downs, and know that valleys don't last always.

I DON'T NEED A COSIGNER FOR MY PRAISE

Many people can only praise in the presence of an audience, these are the people who I say need a cosigner. They need the spiritual leader that taps into their emotions and forces them to reflect on how good God has been to them. They raise their hands because the leader says raise their hands, they clap because the leader says clap. They commune with God only because they were told to. As a praise and worship leader myself, this wears us out. I love to worship with people who are mature enough to just think back on their own what they have been through and it just causes them to bust out in a combustible praise. These are the people that don't need cosigners, but they welcome dance partners. Which are you?

PERSEVERANCE FOR POWER

To persevere means to persist in an idea, purpose, or task despite obstacles. Power means strength, force, might, forceful impact: effectiveness. Just as in a physical workout, resistance builds muscle, so it is in the spiritual realm. The more that you press through opposition, the more spiritual muscles you begin to form. Spiritual muscles are exhibited through the medium of faith. There is a great exchange that happens in the life of a believer. God gives us beauty for ashes, joy for mourning, and a list of other things to include power for perseverance.

SEED, TIME, AND HARVEST

A negative word spoken to a child becomes a seed that, in time, will turn into an adult with low self-esteem. When we pray, we pray for results. We ask for oak trees, but God answers with acorns. God is a God of seed, and no matter what the words are, they always produce something. When God wants to bring forth deliverance, he will sometimes use the foolishness of preaching. God's word is a seed and when he wants to produce, he does so with his word. What are you saying to your children? What are you saying to your loved ones? Most importantly what are you saying to yourself? Remember your words are seeds, even when you speak them to yourself, and it's only a matter of time that they become the harvest which is the reality that you created for yourself.

THE HATCHING OF THE ANOINTED ONE

Have you ever looked at the lifecycle of an animal and likened it to our spiritual experiences. I have, and one of them that I looked at was the bird. The birthing process of a bird can be very intriguing. There are three main threats to their lives before they are even fully hatched. One of them is people. In the spiritual realm people are the naysayers. They want to handle you and often times they mishandle you during the transition that you are making to be one with Christ. The second are predators. In the spiritual realm, these are the people who want to eat you alive with expectations (often, many of which are not biblical). Finally birds also face the risk of losing habitat, which means they are displaced through the removal of the nests. In the spiritual realm, this is you being out of church and you have no one to cover or protect you. This is a very dangerous place to be. If you want to hatch properly, you have to overcome the obstacles that you are prone to face, but don't get discouraged. Just understand that if God is for you, he is more than the world against you.

MEOLOGY 911

Many people think that when you get saved that your problems are all over, but the truth of the matter is that this point is where the problems begins. Why do I say that? I'm glad you asked. There are struggles that start to take place; a struggle between where you've been and where you're going. There is a struggle of doing too much and not doing enough or not doing anything. You holler for help, but no one hears you. They don't see your struggle to get free. They fail to see that sometimes their pressure that they apply for you to have it together, only turn you off, can shut you down, and sometimes even make you weaker. See Meology 101 is the course that comes between salvation and deliverance, but 911 comes after deliverance, but before judgement. There are prerequisites to this course;

- Salvation
- Inspiration
- Holy Ghost impartation

The teacher is the convicting power of the Holy Ghost;
The textbook is the Holy Bible;
Daily Field Experiences are required of all enrolled students.

The materials needed are

- A ready mind
- A text book
- A mirror
- Paper

The question is will you sign up for the course?

THE 3-D VISION OF THE PROPHETIC

The 3-D vision of the prophetic explains the eyesight of those who move under the anointing of the prophetic. The first D is that they are able to accurately DISCERN. Discern means to detect visually; to detect with senses other than that of the vision; to comprehend mentally; to perceive separate and distinctly. The second D is to DECIDE. This means that they are able to settle; to determine the conclusion of or issue of; to make up in one's mind. The third D is to DELIVER. To deliver means to surrender; hand over; to set free; to liberate; to give or send forth; to assist in the birth of an offspring; to convey, transfer, utter or communicate. It only makes sense to define prophesy which means to speak or utter by divine inspiration. Putting all of these puzzle pieces together, we can see that the operation of the prophetic is a heavy duty task and should not be taken lightly. For more in depth information on the 5 fold ministry gifts you can purchase my book For the Perfecting of the Saints: The 5 Fold Ministry Gifts and What They Mean to You!

THE KEYS TO LIVING ABUNDANTLY

If you plan to live abundantly in your life, there are just a few things that you have to do. You have to soar in the spirit and keep your minds on heavenly things. You have to ignore anything other than God's word. You have to understand that you run the risk of being persecuted by the spiritually ignorant. You can't expect them to see things the same as you do. Finally you have to release the past and other weights that so easily beset us. This is the process to living an abundant life. Are you ready?

IT'S ALL IN THE DASH

Whenever you go to the cemetery, it is so interesting that there are always some new arrivals. The headstone counts increase, however, the headstones vary in sizes, shapes, colors and pictures. Though there is a variance in these elements, there are some things that are always going to be the same. There is going to be a birthdate, a death date but most importantly they all have a dash in the middle. The dash or hyphen represents all that has happened in the life of that individual and no matter how long or short their life was the dash is always the same length. The most significant matter of life is what happens in the dash. The problem is that there are two people who want to write your story: God and the devil. God had to write the mess on one page so he can write the miracle on the next. So when you find yourself getting discouraged when you see the messiness of this page, find enough strength to turn the page and get to the miracle because it will make the mess all worth it.

WHO GOD IS?

Know who God is in the fullness of his being so that way you can use his proper name as the resource that you need in your various seasons.

El-Shaddai- All Sufficient
Jehovah Jireh- Provider
El Rafa- Healer
El Niecy-Redeemer
El Baracadas- Sanctifier
El Shaloh-God of Peace
Sekunah-Righteousness
Rene-Sheppard
Shama- Everywhere

God is everything and besides him there is none other. Many of us have heard that he is a mother to the motherless, a father to the fatherless, lawyer in the courtroom, and a doctor in the sick room. That is all fine and good but at the end of the day, who is he really to you?

THE TRUTH OF THE MATTER

The truth of the matter is that many of our issues come in the fact that we simply have to change our vocabulary about the issues that we are going through. Sometimes we honestly just speak defeat over ourselves knowingly and unknowingly. Change your vocabulary to speak the hard truth of the matter that you are going through.

Change "can't" to "unwilling"
Change "problem" to "divine opportunity"
Change "hard" to "challenging"
Change "want" to "desire"
Change "single" to "ready to experience"
Change "broke" to "temporarily out of cash"
Change "by myself" to "with myself"
Change "I'm afraid" to "I'm not clear"

Your issue is all in your verbiage. What is it that you are currently going through? Tell yourself this declaration;

"Yesterday I though _____was a problem. Today I believe_____is a divine opportunity."

Change your verbiage!

677

Day 340

A TIME OF REFLECTION

As we are coming to the close of another year, this is the time that I like to reflect not only on the current year, but I also like to reflect on my life. Here are the questions that I dare you to ask yourself.

- What have I done this year?
- What have I learned?
- How am I using what I learned?
- What do I want now?
- Where do I go from here?

These are vital questions to recalibrate and re-center yourself about matters of the heart, as well as your desires. Don't make another resolution until you resolve and reassess your current situation.

GOOD INTENTIONS DON'T IMPRESS GOD!

One of the most valuable lessons that I learned in my life is that good intentions on your part don't impress God. I want to share a short story to this testimony that happened to me. One day God had told me to start a personal fast on February 1st. I received specific instructions as to what to do to include writing down all the things that I believed God for in this season. God had made me a few promises for this season, and that just fueled my excitement. So much so, that I started the fast a little over a week early. I started strong and I was doing well then my body started to experience challenges. One day, I heard the Lord say to revisit my list of instructions that he had given me in reference to the fast. As I looked at the instructions, I began crossing off my list the things that I had already completed and the promises that were already coming to pass. I was so excited I began to increase the parameters of my fast thinking ignorantly that it would make my results greater, I guess. Finally my body crashed and I fell into a depression. I didn't want to go to church, I didn't desire to be around people, and it seemed as though everything was going wrong. My Pastor and I had a conversation about me and what he said to me dropped in my spirit like a ton of bricks. He told me that perhaps I was going through what I went through because I was disobedient. Disobedient? I haven't eaten my regular diet in weeks! I haven't continued in my regular routine in weeks? How could he possibly come to this conclusion? He went on to ask me questions about my directions for my fast, and I shared them with him and pointed out all of my disobedience. I had never been so lovingly corrected in all of my life. What did I learn from that experience? I learned not to get trapped in my emotions, and to obey the voice of God to the letter. I want to pass this lesson on to you because truly it was a hard pill to swallow!

Day 342

LIFE LESSONS

There are some lessons that I had to learn in my life that fall under no certain category, but they have enabled me to live a more purposeful life that is decreased in aggravation, but increased in elevation. Life lessons are those nuggets that you get when you take time to sincerely reflect on what you are trying to do.

I just want to share a few of them with you during this time of reflection.

- ❖ Close the door to the past
- ❖ Refuse to let anyone send you back to where you came from- no more backtracking
- ❖ If you can submit, you will go further than your teacher
- ❖ You will only receive it when it doesn't matter anymore
- ❖ Every step I took in life, I lost folks
- ❖ There are some places that you can't preach because they are not ready for your capacity

What are some random life lessons you have learned thus far?

Day 343

MAKE THE CONNECTIONS

Your praise is likely to be directly related to your former pain. Understand that the greater the pain, the greater the praise. If you have never been bound, you have no idea how good it feels to be free. Make the connections in your life today and move in those connections. When you make connections such as the ones that I just pointed out to you, you are more readily able to accept the challenges that life brings. God doesn't make mistakes and he is very intentional in him methods. Yield to him and watch God work!

Day 344

WHO AM I?

What does the Bible say about you?

It says;

- ➤ You are fearfully and wonderfully made!
- ➤ You are made by God!
- ➤ You are made in his image!
- ➤ All that he made (including you) is good!
- ➤ You are more than a conqueror!

Yes, there are scripture references to all of these, but I want you to get the revelation and make these words your personal declaration. See scriptures are great and wonderful, but the impact comes when you began to make the declarations a regular part of your daily speech. Speak over yourself starting now!

WORSHIP IS...

Worship has nothing to do with religion, but everything to do with relationship. Worship is where you can be in a room full of people and still feel as though there is no one else in the room but you and God. Worship is where there is only an audience of one, which is the father himself. Worship is where you don't care about notes, tunes or melodies; you are just completely lost in the presence of God. Worship is…! Worship is the ability to just think of who God is to you, and it has nothing to do with material things, but everything to do with who he is in your life, and how he has loved you with and undying love. How he made a way out of no way. How he kept you, even when you didn't want to be kept. Just writing this has me in place where I am ready to enter in…Get into a place of worship and find refuge there from everything that you are going through.

THE PROPER PROCEDURE FOR A PRESSURED SITUATION!

Sometimes when we go through we have a tendency to forget the proper procedures for handling such an adverse situation. We complain to others, when we should be complaining to God. We confide in others, when we should only confide in God. The final step of the procedure is the one that moves God the most; you should commend God, and move in faith as though the situation is already handled. This, my friends, is the proper procedure for handling a pressured situation.

How to Handle Adversarial Advances

I always tell the parents of the students in my class that, after being an educator for so long, there really is a method to my madness. Experience teaches us how to handle certain situations, especially when the plan of attack is predictable and follows a normal pattern. So it is with the enemy. With this truth in mind, there is a strategy that one can follow to handle the attacks of the enemy and because his methods don't change you can practice overcoming them until it becomes second nature. The first thing that one must do is recognize what they are up against. Recognize the person or the entity that we are working against. It's the same spirit; he just used different mediums to get to you. Recognize that he does the same attack, he just practices with different people, his plan is pretty predictable as well, and his patterns never really change. The second thing that we have to do is resist the temptation to react. We have to guard our minds, our words, and of course our deeds. Thirdly, we have to remain in the face of God throughout the ordeal. Lastly, we have to remember who we are in Christ, and know that no matter what it looks like right now; no weapon formed against us shall prosper. Now go and be victorious!

Day 348

CAN YOU RECEIVE GOD'S GIFTS

There are a number of promises that God made us in the Bible. Though there a number of promises, they are all rooted on what I call "The 5 Gifts from God." First of all you have to understand the difference between a promise and a gift. A gift is the foundational premise that all promises are birthed from. Those 5 gifts are love, eternal life, faith, joy, and peace. Notice a few things about these gifts. None of them can be purchased. They all are of the innate qualities that start from the inside and exhibit themselves in many ways on the outside. Here is the question will you receive these gifts or will you keep allowing the enemy to steal them from you?

Day 349

RELEASE THE PAST

The number one method to personal success is to release the past. When I used to reach for greatness, there was always something holding me back? I used to blame my weakness on everything else externally, and then I realized that there was a root to the routine of failure, low self-esteem and the lack of confidence that I once had. That root was my past. What my mom said to me, what my brother did to me. What the world classified me as, and so on and so forth. Then I received a challenge from the Lord that changed my life forever. He simply asked me would I dare to release my past. I asked him how that was possible when there was so much wrong done to me and he gave me three words;

- Person
- Problem
- Prescription

I had to realize that I was not that person that they tried to label me as. Next, I had to understand that their insecurities were their problem and not mine. God gave me the perfect prescription to break those chains of bondage that kept me bound, chase after him and him alone.

LIVE IN OBEDIENCE

Do you understand that partial obedience is still complete disobedience? If God tells you to walk five miles, you are obedient in your walking, but if you only walk three miles, you are still being disobedient, and there will still be consequences to pay. The reason why complete obedience is the only way is because there is always a reason for every season and situation that God allows in your life. Using the same five mile analogy, let's say you only walked three miles when he said five. There may be someone at mile four that needs to have an encounter and experience with you, but in your disobedience, they are stuck in their mess because you didn't complete the course. Choose today to live in obedience: complete obedience as there could be lives on the line awaiting you.

SUCCESSFUL LEADERS

Successful leaders act on God's word at all times and at all costs. One thing that I have always said, no matter how many times I am asked, I do not desire to be a Pastor! Being in leadership is hard enough, but to be a pastor is a whole other level of faith that I honestly don't feel as though I possess. As a leader, some of our struggles and expectations are the same though the methodology may be different. You can expect some fake friends: ones that are around as long as the lights are on you. They are hanging out only to see if they will get their spotlight opportunity. In that same vein, you can expect to be betrayed. One of the reasons for this is because Jesus was betrayed, and if they did it to him, you better believe you are not exempt. Lastly, you can expect doubt. Not everyone is going to sing your praises. One thing that I hear Pastors say all the time is trust my heart, not my head. The reason is that we, as followers, have to trust that their heart chases after God exclusively, because there are times that he will give them orders that make sense to no one and probably not even them. If you cannot trust the heart of the man and/or woman of God that you support, you may need to find a new place to worship.

THE ALL KNOWING GOD!

We have to be confident in the relationship that we are in with Christ. This means that we have to trust him in all of our ways. We must seek him first and trust that in our seeking that he will be meeting our needs. We have to understand that in order for us to be successful we have to keep in mind that we have kingdom business to tend to and in order to do it effectively; we have to have balance in our lives, to include times of rest and relaxation. We have to know and believe that he gives us back more than what we give and that it is in our weary, cloudy days that he directs us. Understand that things are going to happen, but we must first be confident in our King!

HELP! I'M IN LABOR

As a woman, labor pains are the worst pains that one will ever encounter, for most of us anyway. Labor pains are the measuring sticks to which we compare all other pains to. When we look in the spiritual realm, we have to understand that labor pains are designed by God to kill and deliver. The labor pains that we encounter in the spiritual realm are those to kill our flesh, and deliver a relationship with Christ that will be untouchable. When we get saved, we should become very protective of our relationship with him. We don't allow anyone to handle us any kind of way as we encounter and pursuit a more personal relationship with him. Don't be afraid of the labor pains to come. Find you a midwife for every area in your life that you go through. That person will become the person that has already mastered what you are going through or about to go through and they walk you through the process. They do so successfully because they humbly, yet successfully came through their process with a powerful testimony that they don't mind sharing. Go through your labor so that you can become the midwife to someone else.

WHERE ARE THE REAL MEN?

What is a real man? This question can be answered by ten different people in ten different ways, but from a revelatory standpoint is what I am going to use to base my answer on. Coming from someone who has been married on more than one occasion, all for different reasons, I feel well able and qualified to answer, but first let me share my testimony. The first time I got married I was 18 years old. He was my high school sweetheart and we had already been through so much together including a miscarriage when I was 15. We had a successful pregnancy when I was sixteen which was my daughter. I married him because as a child I made myself a promise and laid it before the Lord that the man I had children with would be my husband. To be exact my exact words were, "Lord, when I get big, I want to have a boy and a girl, just like my mom, but both of them will have the same father, and he is going to be my husband, and we are going to be married forever. I spoke from this place because of my painful childhood experiences. Well my mom passed away when I was 18, and I was lost. So ignorantly I married him to keep my promise to myself, but also because I thought that this act would keep us together forever. I had another baby a few months after marriage. This baby came with his own set of challenges which took a toll on our relationship, and to save myself and my children I left. Then I moved to Texas and met what I thought to be the man of my dreams. He was supportive of me and my children and loved us dearly. Though he was 12 years my senior, our relationship had its own set of struggles. For the longest time, I felt obligated to marry him because he had done so much for my family, especially my son who longed for his dad. Husband number 2 stepped right in and filled the gap to the best of his ability and my childish way of showing gratitude was to be his wife. I went through several seasons in my life trying to chase external happiness in hopes that it would heal me internally and give me joy. Epic fail! When I returned from my season of riotous living the church made me feel as though I had to be married to prove a point. So ignorantly I literally married a stranger who was very abusive and deceitful. It was after that last failed marriage that was actually annulled that I threw myself into God and told him my desires and he led me through scriptures of real men. Men who loved their wives as Christ loved the church, no matter what they had to do to prove it. From all of this I have learned this truth; a real man stands with and for his family while he leads and covers them in every manner.

Day 355

THE SEVEN DEADLY SINS OF SISTERHOOD!

Sisterhood is a wonderful thing when done right. Done right, meaning that they have a mutual respect for each other that cannot be toiled with in any manner. I have had the same best friend for almost twenty years if not more. Many people encounter us and marvel at our relationship. The most common question is what is the secret? Well here it is, we don't partake in what I call the 7 Deadly Sins of Sisterhood which are;

- Betrayal
- Manipulation
- Judgement
- Envy
- Gossip
- Competition
- Resentment

When you have a relationship that is free of these sins, how could it not be a success?

ABUNDANT LIVING

When we speak of living abundantly, many people interpret that differently, and their interpretation can be based on a lot of different things. Abundant living comes free from restriction, but not of obstacles. Abundant living is the ability to be able to soar in the spirit while ignoring the opposition. You expect opposition because you know that elevation comes as a result of turbulence. You accept that risk and go in with the mindset of overcoming it all. The most important part of abundant living is the ability to release. Release yourself from the bondages that hold you. Release the people who have wronged you and never came to get it right. Release the responsibility of those who owe you in any manner, but never came to reconcile. This, my friends, is abundant living.

THE INTERNAL INVESTIGATION

Why can't we forgive ourselves when we commit the act of being human and making a mistake. Honestly, look internally and see where the issue is. Could it be that we think that we are equal to God and free from mistakes and issues? Or could it be that we can't handle the disappointment that comes with the reality of our first option. Maybe it is because we are in the state of denial. We deny the fact that we are truly human and will make mistakes and sometimes we may even make the same mistake more than once. With that in mind, perhaps we don't forgive ourselves because we know that we plan to do it again. This is a basis for the term insanity; doing the same thing and expecting different results. Did you ever think that maybe we are victims of low self-esteem so we do not think ourselves to be able to perform above our mistakes? We say things like, this is just who I am. Either way, when we perform an internal investigation and we authentically seek the face of God about the matter, he will show us the magnitude and the multitude of our sins. Will you dare to do an internal investigation today?

WHAT DOES IT MEAN TO FORGIVE MYSELF?

Forgiving ourselves is one of the hardest tasks that we will ever encounter. Shall I say true self forgiveness? When you choose to let yourself off the hook there are a few things that happen as a result of that process;

You envelope the expression of his love,
You exceed your present existence,
You excel in your efforts for the eternal,
You accept redemption,
You receive the restoration,

When you can successfully forgive yourself, it makes it easier to forgive others, and makes like a lot easier to live. Start today and forgive yourself as well as forgive others, because you can't have one without the other.

THE SIGNIFICANCE OF REMAINING
IN THE SECRET PLACE

Psalms 91 tells us all about the secret place, but I want to tell you from a revelatory standpoint the significance of remaining in the secret place. The first thing is that you have to get there and stay there. In that place, a personal relationship with Christ is formed. As a result of that relationship, deliverance takes place. Deliverance takes place because you feel safe in the secret place because there is no one else there but you and your creator. Are you really able to hide anything from the person who created you: the person who knows the number of hairs on your head? It's in that place that he blesses you with a spiritual ignore button that you can use to ignore outside elements that will take you out of your place of peace. Beware now, because others will hate you, but you have to stay in that place. Because of the close proximity of you and God, revelation comes more readily because you can't help but begin to see things the way that God sees them. You also remain protected and you don't look for anyone else to aid you because God becomes your personal first aid provider. He will exhort you and give you confidence to overcome obstacles while you walk away with new knowledge. There is also a consistent line of communication that is opened between you and God that solidifies your relationship with him. Now tell me again why you won't get into the secret place?

Day 360

ARE YOU IN IT TO WIN IT OR WILL YOU CONTINUE IN DEFEAT?

As we end the year and come to a closing of this devotional there are a number of powerful words that you have encountered. At this point, I have to stop and ask you "Are you ready to take your encounter now to an experience?" See an encounter is just the ability to partake in a thing without expecting any change or real result. An experience is where you participate in a thing with a spirit of expectancy and that expectation is rooted in change. This is the place that the question is asked, "Are you in it to win it or will you continue in defeat?" What is your answer?

THAT WAS THEN, THIS IS NOW, SO NOW WHAT?

I love it when people try to remind me of where I have been and what I have done. It is amazing to me to see God work through their ill intents. He lets me know that I am still okay and I am still his. It wasn't long ago that these acts used to really bother me and get under my skin. Now that God has matured me my response is, "That was then, this is now, so now what?"

Day 362

THINK YOUR WAY THROUGH THE GATE OF DECISION!

Think on these decision nuggets;

- To not make a decision is a decision,
- Nothing that your enemy does over you can have an effect on you
- Destinies are forged in the furnace of real decisions
- Faith is incubated in the fires of apprehension (take a step to take a risk)
- God will hide your need and allow your enemy to perceive you to be more powerful than you are
- Transition- you are too far out to be in, and too far in to go back out

What causes bad decisions?

- Limited information causes bad decisions
- When Past Experiences control current decisions
- Surrounding yourself with foolish people
- Failing to take cues from God

This information is designed to assist you in thinking your way through your storms! Knowledge is power. Power brings about perseverance. Perseverance brings about performance. Think!

ENTER INTO BATTLE WITH CONFIDENCE!

How does one win every single battle that they enter? While it may be impossible to win every single one, even if you lose a battle you can still win the war. Here are your strategies;

1. Identify the bully
2. Receive instruction on how to handle the bully
3. Allow God to intervene!

While you are using these strategies, think on these things;

*   Remember "them"- those who are threatened by your success
*   When they can't get to you, they will get to the ones closest to you
*   They will even join in with their enemies against you
*   Fear is not an option
*   Don't let fear keep you from doing the right thing
*   Don't let fear keep you from doing your best
*   Don't let fear keep you from hearing the word of God

This is how you not only enter into battle with confidence, but also the mind frame that one should have while in battle. The question is do you have the confidence to do it?

DON'T JUST SIT THERE DO SOMETHING!

Many people get into church and want to complain about the things that are and maybe are not getting done, especially if they are not done the way that "they" believe that things should be done. The question is, "What are you doing?" I am not sure what your answer is, but here is what it should be... You should desire to find your place in the body. You should be trying to discover how to operate in the spirit of excellence in that thing that you feel that you were called to do. Once you figure that part out, then you should start displaying it for the world to see. Whatever you do, don't just sit there do something!

REJECT THE PITFALLS

There are a number of spiritual pitfalls that we fall in that could potentially blow our witness, if exposed. Those pitfalls are issues such as;

- Trying to be undercover Christians
- Trying to ignore the pitfalls
- Being at a spiritual standstill
- Holding on to pitfalls in the form of baggage
- Rejecting the wrong things

These are all of the problems that we go through that we have to ensure that we are ready to tackle and address in order to experience the freedom that God has for us. There are solutions to these potential issues which are;

- To illuminate the issues through the word of God,
- Identify what your personal pitfalls are,
- Understand the importance in realizing that all things work together for the good,
- Imitate Christ when you do fall, knowing that he is our ultimate example

Remember this that pitfalls show us what we are really made of!

IT IS FINISHED!

Why is it that we compartmentalize the Bible and the occurrences that happened? What do I mean? I am glad that you asked! What did you think about when you read the title of today's devotional? Many people would look at it and think of the seven last sayings of Christ that we have reserved for the Resurrection Season. Others may have looked at it and thought that I was celebrating the fact that this book is FINALLY DONE! There are so many interpretations to this title and the truth of the matter is that it means all of the above mentioned and then some. See I said when I wrote my first book that I wanted to write a book every year for the rest of my life. I did it for three years and then life happened. I was in and out of bad relationships. I survived cancer. I started my professional career in education, and did a number of other things. This book is representative of the resurrection of my call, will, and desire not just for me, but for Christ. This book serves as my rededication to my craft, my recommitment to my dreams and when I say it is done, I mean it.

The excuses are done!
The sob stories are done!
The procrastination is done!
The insecurities are done!

The self-doubt is done!
The struggles that I allowed to stop me are done!

Am I saying that I think that I am exempt from issues of life and that the rest is smooth sailing? NO! But I am saying that I will no longer let anyone or anything come between my goals and I again!

EPILOGUE

I hope it blessed you to read this book as much as it blessed me to write it. From this experience, I hope that you have learned the importance of taking time for yourself. Remember that when we ask God to fill our cups, he does so in our personal time of devotion and the overflow is for others. Too often we give our filling to others and we walk around emotionally, spiritually and financially bankrupt after giving our all to others. I hope this devotional has gotten you into the practice of taking time to devote to yourself and to Christ. Though this book is done, don't let your devotional time end, keep it up. You deserve it and so does God!

AFTERWORD BY
LADY CHERYL STALLINGS

Dr. Jennifer Gilbert's "365 Revelatory Words for any Given Day" is an amazing collaboration of devotion, wisdom, and hope. The transparency birthed from her personal struggles, battles, and victories have been transcribed, awaking one's own challenges and accomplishments on this journey through life. Each day gives a fresh perspective of God's expectations and love for his children. This book, addresses the truths and dispels the belief of many victims of their own circumstances, who like many have conditioned themselves to believe such clichés such as" life doesn't get any better than this, so deal with it"," you will never amount to anything"," or you're fighting a losing battle". All for which we know are Satan's deceptive and cunning way to keep one defeated in the mind. Through, Dr. Gilbert's liberating daily journal the sentiments of the heart of God according to Mathew 11:28-30 offers hope, encouragement, support, and guidance to all readers. This enriching, motivating, and inspiring book is a must have tool to add to any believers spiritual toolbox as we daily navigate through life.

Lady Cheryl Stallings
Perfecting Praise Community Church
Houston, TX

ABOUT THE AUTHOR

Dr. Jennifer Gilbert, ED.D.

Minister Jennifer Gilbert is a well-known preacher, teacher, prophet and praise and worship leader throughout Texas and the surrounding areas. Born in Lawton, Oklahoma but raised worldwide by a military family while overcoming very serious and personal issues she answered her call to God at the tender age of 9, but due to the oppression of man and their opinions, she did not fully walk in her calling until 2002. She is an honored high school graduate of Bradwell Institute in Hinesville, Georgia, Class of 1993. She completed the beginning of her college career with a High Honored Associates in Child Development and Business Administration, and has completed her Bachelors in the same areas of expertise at Tarleton State University. She also completed her Masters in

Adult Education and Training at the University of Phoenix. She has her Ph.D. in Christian Education from Northwestern Theological Seminary School and nearly completed her Educational Doctorates (Ed.D) from the University of Phoenix with all but her dissertation done.

Minister Gilbert has served faithfully in many positions both past and present. Some of those positions are or have been: Head of Pastors' Support, Lead Intercessor, Youth Pastor, Head of Youth Drama Ministry, Head of Youth Mime Ministry, Choir Member and assistant choir director, Pres. Of the YPD (young people's division), Praise and Worship Leader, Overseer of the financial committee, outreach ministry, evangelism and administration.

Minister Gilbert's greatest loves, second to God, are her two children, Damaria and J'Donte (J.J.) Henderson who reside in Texas as they pursue their own collegiate careers and personal aspirations, but more so her grandson Ethan J'Cean Henderson.

Her famous quote is, "There is power in perseverance through painful persecution." She coined this quote during the painful persevering pursuit of her deliverance from years of abusive relationships and other strongholds that were overcome by the grace of God and radical perseverance against all odds.

She believes that her ultimate gift is to teach, preach and share a tangible Jesus; one whose heart can be touched through authentic praise and worship, individually and corporately, and through honest **relationship, not religion.**

She is embarking upon this work through her books, "Churchin' Ain't Easy" released 2011 and "…And Deliver Us from People…" released in 2012, her book, "For the Perfecting of the Saints: The Five Biblical Ministry Gifts and What They Mean to You" released in 2014 along with a number of other books to come in the year of 2017. She has also released her gospel cd single "Can I Just Be Me?" a full length gospel cd entitled "Love Covers All" with business partner CaCean Ballou. She is also the owner and CEO of JGM Educational Consultants that seeks to assist in furthering the education and ensuring the educational success of students of all ages from Pre-K to Post Grads both secularly and in religion. She is also a committed educator and has a passion for writing that is made evident through all of her literary ventures. To God be all the glory!

INDEX

Printed in the United States
By Bookmasters